Two Books A

I.

A Comparison of the Roman and Evangelical Churches

also known as

A Brief and Careful Description. (1629)

by

Nicolaus Hunnius

Superintendent at Lübeck

II.

A Catholic Answer to the Heretical Question of the Jesuits: Where Was the True Religion and Church before the Time of Luther? (1627)

by

Balthasar Meisner

Doctor and Professor of Holy Scripture at Wittenberg

translated by Paul A. Rydecki

• REPRISTINATION PRESS•

Dedicated in memory of Rev. Dr. Richard J. Dinda

Published in 2017

REPRISTINATION PRESS
716 HCR 3424 E
MALONE, TEXAS 76660

www.repristinationpress.com

ISBN 1-891469-74-6

Table of Contents

4

A Comparison of the Roman and Evangelical Churches

also known as

A Brief and Careful Description,

from Which a Good-Hearted Reader May Judge Between the Roman and Evangelical Churches.

Drawn from the Word of God

by

Nicolaus Hunnius

Superintendent at Lübeck

1629

Third Edition

Wittenberg

1697

Dear Christian Reader,

The very thing about which the apostle Paul once complained (2 Tim. 3:6), namely, that seductive teachers were sneaking into households to take simple people captive, was also taking place at the time of Pastor Nicolaus Hunnius. For at that time, a sly character arose and had a little book published in Osnabrück entitled: *A Brief and Careful Report from Which a Good-Hearted Reader May Easily Come to a Knowledge of the Truth, to be read among the people of Lübeck, in which the author set forth his understanding of the entire matter in eleven combative articles*. Pastor Hunnius offered his own little book in response to these articles and, by applying the Word of God to all points, highlighted the important warning: that a person neither could nor should by any means be associated with the Roman Church. But since this little book began to disappear, so that one could hardly find a copy anywhere, and yet many at the present time have been searching for it, therefore it is now being republished for the benefit and instruction of all.

A.D. 1697

The First Chief Point.

The Undeniably True Church and Faith.

[1][1] It will be proven that the Roman Church and faith (as it exists today) are not Christian, genuine, and true, because:

I. She removes from the Christian Church the means whereby she is to receive the salutary divine doctrine;

II. She forces an errant and deceptive means upon her;

III. She deprives her of the true means of salvation;

IV. She provides her with other, useless means;

V. She leads her astray to an ungodly way of life;

VI. She plunges her back into the old Judaism, heathenism, and heresies;

VII. She robs her of all comfort;

VIII. She deprives her of Christian freedom and drives her into harsh slavery;

IX. She accomplishes everything by means of hypocrisy;

X. And she binds Christians to such a head as cannot be the head of Christians.

All this will now be further explored.

[2] (I) The Roman Church removes from Christians the means whereby they should receive the salutary divine doctrine; namely, the Holy Scripture, by which God teaches men and [a2]

1 Bracketed numbers are paragraphs in the original work. Hunnius used these numbers for cross-referencing within this work, and therefore they have been retained.

2 Hunnius utilizes a system of notes within his text, designating them

equips them to stand [b] against Satan. For the Roman Church considers the Holy Scripture:

1. To be useless for Christian doctrine, as if it were [c] a mere piece of paper, [d] a wax nose, [e] a lead weight, and [f] a dead letter, written with ink on parchment or paper, like a sheathe into which a sword of steel or of lead or of wood may be placed, as something that one can interpret however he wishes. Therefore, they imagine that the Scripture avails little [g] without the testimony of the Church, and they liken it [h] to Aesop's Fables.

2. To be harmful to the Christian Church, since [i] there would be many fewer heretics if the Holy Scripture didn't exist at all. Thus, because of [j] the great harm that can come from reading the Bible, [k] not everyone is permitted to read it.

3. Therefore, she also commonly [l] forbids the laity to read the Holy Scripture or [m] to fortify themselves with it against the devil's attacks.

(a) John 5:39; Luke 16:29; 2 Tim. 3:15. (b) Eph. 6:17; Mat. 4:4, 7, 10. (c) Coster. Enchir. c. 1. p. 43. (d) Pigh. de pot. Papae contr. 3. (e) Pigh. de Hier. Eccl. lib. 1. c. 2. (f) Coster. Enchirid. cap. 1. p. 44. (g) Hosius de autorit. script. p. 562. c. (h) Pistorius contra Mentzer. falso 898. (i) Gretser. defens. 1. controv. lib. 4. c. 12. pag. 1842. a. (j) Lancell. haeretic. quare 16. §. 12. Bejerl. conc. select. 19. p. 370. (k) Less. de Antichr. demonstr. 15. p. 135. Hack wider Tossan. Frag. 2. Cap. 28. (l) lib. 5. decretal. tit. 7. de haereticis, cap. 12. cum ex injuncto. (m) Hosius de Autorit. Script. pag. 543. b. c.

[3] (II) The Roman Church forces upon Christians other means from which they should draw Christian doctrine—means that, nevertheless, have not been commanded them by God; of which they cannot be certain; nor can they build their faith and salvation upon them with certainty; which are, furthermore, rejected by the pope himself. They are:

---

with superscripted letters. We have retained his system of notation.

[4] (1) [a] The pope, although he either teaches Christians nothing at all or merely instructs them with spiritual laws which contain little about the articles of faith, etc. In addition, the pope himself only wishes to have his decrees considered in those areas [b] about which the Holy Scriptures establish nothing certain. Furthermore, he only allows his teaching to avail where [c] it does not run contrary to natural law, or [d] where it thoroughly agrees with common law. For this reason, [e] the pope himself must often wonder whether his statutes are right or wrong, since [f] some of them he makes up, others he [g] distorts and changes, etc.

(a) decretal. tit. 2. de constit. c. 13. quoniam. (b) dist. 11. 3. 7. in his rebus. (c) dist. 9. c. 11. sana quippe. (d) lib. 2. deret. tit. 22. de fide Instrum. c. 8. Pastoralis. (e) ibid. (f) dist. 19. c. 9. Anastasius. (g) caus. 33. quaest. 7. c. 17. uxor a viro. c. 18. quod proposuisti.

[5] (2) The Fathers, that is, [a] the ancient teachers of the Church, without whom [b] no one can be certain of a single article of Holy Scripture. And yet the pope himself must confess that [c] one should only accept from the writings of the Fathers that which is entirely certain and [d] agrees with the truth. In other cases, [e] each one is free to depart from them.

(a) Hack 1. frag. Cap. 3. p. 37. seq. (b) ibid. 2. Frag Beschluss / p. 695. (c) dist. 9. cap. 3. noli meis. (d) ibid. cap. 9. noli frater. (e) ibid. cap. 10. neque.

[6] (3) The Councils, that is the assemblies of the churches, which, as [a] the supreme court of the Church, cannot err, and, therefore, should be considered [b] practically equal to the Gospels and [c] on par with the Holy Scriptures. And yet, since the pope must admit that [d] the Councils also form conclusions that contradict one another, and since it is clear that they have, at times, formed wicked conclusions, or conclusions that are contrary to the papacy, the Roman Church does not allow itself to be bound by these conclusions, because they are uncertain.

(a) Tann. part. 2. Anat. dem. 10. §. 222. seq. (b) dist. 16. c. 2. sancta octo. (c) Badische 6. Motiv. p. 354. (d) dist. 50. c. 28. Domino, caus. 33. quaest. 2. c. 11. hoc ipsum quod.

[7] I will demonstrate this with only two examples. In [a] the Elibertine Council it was determined:

1. He who [b] attains his years and, after his baptism, makes an offering to idols, [c] murders another through witchcraft, is [d] driven again to fornication after repenting of adultery, [e] accuses a bishop or priest of a great crime without being able to prove it, etc. — to all such people the use of the Holy Supper shall be denied, even on their deathbed.

2. There [f] shall be no images in the churches.

3. Rulers [g] shall not enter the church during the period of their government.

4. No one [h] shall light a lamp in the graveyards during the day, so as not to disturb the holy souls.

(a) Tom. 1. Concil. pag. 282. seq. (b) Can. 1. (c) Can. 6. (d) Can. 7. (e) Can. 75. (f) Can. 36. (g) Can. 56. (h) Can. 34.

[8] The [a] Council Gangrense[3] offers these decrees:

1. If anyone [b] condemns the wife of a priest, as if she could not enter into the kingdom of God as long as she dwells legitimately with her husband, let him be anathema.

2. If anyone [c] extols his virginity over against a married couple, let him be anathema.

3. Any [d] children who abandon their parents under the pretense of worshiping God, let them be anathema.

If these Councils are followed, whatever will become of Christendom and the papacy?

3 That is, the Synod of Grangra, which met in A.D. 340 and condemned the Manichaeans.

(a) Tom. 1. Concil. pag. 289 seq. (b) Can. 1. (c) Can. 9. 10. (d) Can. 16.

[9] (4) Tradition, that is, the unwritten Word of God, which is [a] treated as highly important. And yet, since it is probable that [b] false doctrine has also been lauded as tradition, even as [c] the Pharisees and [d] other heretics have praised their own error as being the unwritten Word, and since the papacy itself does not know if a doctrine should be passed down as traditions or not and, therefore, cannot risk placing them formally in [e] a registry, nor can they point to [f] any definite, particular feature whereby a person can know which traditions are true and which are false, one can easily conclude that traditions are an inept means of teaching Christians.

(a) Bellarm. lib. 4. de Verb. Dei cap. 4. seq. (b) Grets. defens. 1. lib. 4. cap. 7. pag. 1669. c. (c) Mat. 19:2 ff. (d) Gretser. l. d. pag. 1669. c. d. Tanner. diopt. lib. 2. quaest. 4. c. 20. pag. 486. (e) Colloq. Ratisp. Sess. 1. p. 35. Hosius lib. 4. de tradit. pag. 597. b. seq. (f) Bellarm. lib. 4. de verb. Dei. cap. 9.

[10] (5) Special divine revelations, which [a] the pope boldly claims for himself, and yet he testifies that [b] no one can know whether such an inner gift comes from God. Therefore, he [c] commands that no one in the Church shall allow to stand that which has been given through dreams and dubious revelations, since [d] the devil uses these as opportunities to deceive people by feigning a divine appearance. How, then, can they be dependable means of teaching?

(a) Caus. 33. quaest. 3. dist. 2. cap. 15. cum anctam. lib. 4. decretal. tit. 32. de conversat. conjug. cap. 14. ex parte. (b) lib. 1. decretal. tit. 9. de renunciat. cap. 12. nisi cum pridem. (c) de consecrate. dist. 1. cap. 26. placuit, ut altaria. (d) Gretser. defens. 1. append. pag. 1893. seq.

[11] (III) The Roman Church deprives Christians of the true means of salvation.

(1) The chief means of salvation is [a] the merit of Christ. But the Roman Church [b] does not really consider this to be necessary. Although [c] she claims that it is enough to pay for sins, she

thinks that, in truth, [d] Christ has not paid for any sins, but has only [e] acquired for us the ability to gain something by our own works.

(a) Acts 4:12. (b) Peltan. de satisfact. sect. 1. pag. 4. sect. 4. pag. 48. (c) Badische 1. Motiv. pag. 39. 53. (d) Peltan. de satisfact. sect. 10. pag. 134. (e) Idem, sect. 10. pag. 119. Scherer 3. Pred. am. 1. Advents. pag. 17. b.

[12] (2) There are three means of appropriating the merit of Christ: [a] faith, [b] the Holy Scriptures, and [c] the Holy Sacraments. The Roman Church deprives Christendom of faith by turning it into nothing more than a knowledge of history, [d] which the demons also have. At the same time, that special faith by which a Christian [e] confidently appropriates to himself the merit of his Redeemer is [f] most shamefully despised in the Roman Church. It has already been [g] noted above how she takes the Holy Scriptures away from Christians.

(a) Eph. 2:8; Rom. 8:1. (b) Rom. 1:19. (c) Titus 3:5; 1 Pet. 3:21; (d) James 2:19; (e) Luke 7:50; Gal. 2:20. (f) Stapl. Antid. in Act. 5:37, p. 120. in cap. 10:4, p. 160. in c. 13:48, p. 272. (g) num. 2.

[13] The Sacraments are seriously weakened of their benefit in the Roman Church: in part, because she includes as Sacraments things [a] which God has not ordained—indeed, things [b] which God calls unclean, [c] which drive out the Holy Spirit, [d] which hinder prayer and the use of the Holy Supper, [e] which cannot please God, and [f] which are common among the heathen; and in part, because she administers the Sacraments [g] in an unknown language, whereby occasion is given [h] for the desecration of them and for trickery.

(a) Bellarm. lib. 2. de Sacram. cap. 24. seq. (b) caus. 32. quaest. 1. cap. 12. nuptiae terram. (c) caus. 33. quaest. 2. cap. 4. conuubia. (d) caus. 33. quaest. 4. c. 1. sciatis. (e) dist. 82. cap. 2. proposuisti. (f) 1. decretal. tit. 36. de transact. c. 11. Ex parte tua. (g) Bejerl. conc. select. 19. p. 362. (h) Luther. 6. Jehn. Theil. am 88. Blat.

[14] Holy Baptism is dishonored when the Roman Church [a] allows even the bells to be baptized. She ascribes Baptism's efficacy

[b] to the other ceremonies, without which Baptism is said not to cleanse from sins. She ascribes greater power [c] to Confirmation than to Baptism, since Baptism is said [d] not to confer the Holy Spirit [e] upon those who sin after receiving it. She robs it of all its power, and yet, at the same time, she pretends that it serves for the healing even of physical maladies.

(a) Pontifical. edit. Lugdun. anni 1511. f. 154. seq. Bejerl. Conc. select. 44. pag. 799. (b) de consecr. dist. 5. cap. 10. nunquid. (c) de cons. dist. 5. cap. 2. Spiritus sanctus. (d) Bejerl. Conc. select. 41. pag. 763. (e) Staplet. promp. Cath. fest. Ascens. §. 2 pag. 114. 118. de consecrate. dist. 4. cap. 38. non illud.

[15] The Holy Supper is turned into something foreign. (1) The Sacrament is [a] changed into a sacrifice. (2) Where Christ instituted [b] a single administration, the Roman Church [c] makes two: one for the priests, another for the laity. (3) Christ ordained [d] wine for the Sacrament; the Roman Church [e] calls for water to be added, to such an extent that the Sacrament may be administered [f] without any wine at all. (4) Christ [g] gave the Sacrament in two forms; the Roman Church [h] has robbed the laity of one of them. (5) Christ [i] commanded us to eat and to drink; the Roman Church [j] adds processions, [k] adorations, etc. (6) Christ ordained it [l] only for the living; the Roman Church ordains it [m] also for the dead. (7) Christ gave it [n] for His remembrance. In the Roman Church it is greatly abused. It is used [o] to confirm spurious things, as with an oath; [p] to prove one's innocence; [q] to choose rulers and princes; [r] to rescue people from the danger of water; [s] to heal damaged eyes; yes, even [t] to perform secret acts of murder by means of it. (8) Christ distributed it to His disciples [u] after they had eaten. The Roman Church [v] instills a guilty conscience in anyone who does not receive it on an empty stomach. It is not possible for the Christian Church to do such things.

(a) Bell. lib. 1. de Miss. cap. 6. seq. (b) 1 Cor. 11:20. (c) dist. 50. cap. 7. si Epis. cap. 8. si quis. (d) Luke 22:18. (e) de cons. dist. 2. cap. 7. cum omne, cap. 2. sic in sanctific. (f) Bell. lib. 4. de Rom. Pont. cap. 14. §

Quadragesimus. (g) Mat. 26:16, 27. (h) Bell. lib. 4. de Euch. cap. 20. seq. (i) Mat. 26:26, 27. (j) Staplet. Promt. Cathol. de venerate. Sacram. deport. p. 153. (k) Bell. lib. 4. de Euchar. c. 29. (l) 1 Cor. 11:26. (m) 3. decret. tit. 41. de celeb. Miss. cap. 11. cum creatura. de cons. dist. 1. c. 72. visum. (n) 1 Cor. 11:25. (o) Zwing. Theat. p. 1355. a. (p) Caus. 2. quaest. 5. c. 13. saepe contingit. c. 26. si Eposcopi. Zwing. Theat. p. 183. (q) ibid. p. 1355. b. (r) Tann. diopt. l. 2. quaest. 4. c. 20. p. 494. (s) Theat. Zwing. p. 340. a. (t) ibid. p. 466. b. p. 506. b. (u) Luke 22:20. (v) Tolet. lib. 6. cas. consc. c. 15.

[16] The Roman Church directs Christians to such means of salvation as they are unable to attain—means that are neither extolled nor commended to us by God, namely:

(1) The [a] fulfilling of the Law, as [b] something which is deemed possible (contrary [c] to God's Word). (2) [d] Fasting. (3) A [e] harsh and strict life. (4) [f] Monastic vows. (5) [g] Donations and gifts that are made to the churches and cloisters, etc. (6) [h] Pilgrimages to the graves of the saints. (7) [i] Holy water. (8) [j] Making the sign of the cross. (9) [k] Commemorations of the martyrs, who are all supposed to chase away the devil, blot out sin, and give righteousness and salvation. (10) Not to mention that the Roman Church wants to drive out Satan [l] by means of St. John's Gospel and (according to [m] the proclamation of the pontiff) practically all created things that are blessed, such as churches, altars, incense, crosses, burial sites, chrism, salt, oil, water, ashes, vestments, rings, gloves, nuns' veils, etc. All these are supposed to serve for the spiritual welfare of Christians and for the salvation of their souls. The true Christian Church knows nothing about any of this.

(a) Staplet. promt. cathol. Domin. Septuag. §. 3. Domin. Passion. §. 3. (b) Bellar. lib. 4. de justific. cap. 11. seq. (c) Staplet. Antid. in Act. 15:10 pag. 338. (d) Bellarm. lib. 2. de operib. bonis in part. cap. 11. §. Quarto. seq. (e) caus. 33. quaest. 3. dist. 1. cap. 16. qui sanctus. (f) Extravag. Joh. 22. tit. 14. de verb. signif. cap. 5. quia quorundam. (g) caus. 12. quaest. 3. cap. 3. Pontifices. lib. 2. decretal. tit. 2. de foro comp. cap. 16. confessus est. (h) Canon poenit. 40. (i) de consecrate.

dist. 3. cap. 20. aquam. Anton. Marsil. Col. hydragiol. sect. 3. cap. 2. §. 14. (j) Tanner. part. 2. Anat. dem. 3. §. 17. dem. 9. §. 87. (k) Ibid. dem. 3. §. 131. (l) Abrah. Bzov. Annal. Eccles. ann. 1200. §. 20. Anno 1285. §. 17. (m) Lugdun. anno 1511.

[17] (V) The Roman Church leads Christians astray to a godless way of life. This commonly happens when she leads them into sin through [a] indulgences; through [b] the freedom of the priests, whom no one may reproach; through the defense of these same people, so that [c] a person is unwilling to allow them to be shamed for their sins; through the tyrannical compulsion of consciences, who must also fear [d] the unjust judgment of the prelates; through the lust for gold which drives the Roman Church, so that [e] she places a certain gold tax on the grossest sins in order to redeem them, turning [f] godliness into a business. Likewise, she [g] allows each one to choose for himself his own forms of worship, ascribing to them ([h] contrary to God's Word) [i] greater merit than to the forms of service that are commanded by God.

(a) Extrav. comm. lib. 5. tit. 9. de poenit. & remiss. cap. 3. Etsi dominici. c. 5. Etsi dom. (b) dist. 83. c. 2. Nemo. (c) Caus. 2. quaest. 7. cap. 52. criminationes. lib. 5. decretal. tit. 1. de accus. etc. cap. 24. qualiter. cap. 21. Inquisitionis. (d) Caus. 11. quaest. 3. cap. 1. sentential. (e) 5. decretal. tit. 3. de Simon. cap. 39. sicut pro certo. Stadtliche Ausfürung pag. 603. seq. (f) 1 Tim. 6:5. Baron. anno 320. §. 19. seq. (g) Bell. lib. 4. de poenit. c. 4. (h) Mat. 15:0. (i) caus. 33. quaest. 5. cap. 9. qui sitit.

[18] Worship in the Roman Church is [a] treated with contempt, especially against the First Table. It has, at times, been [b] suspended by interdict for many years at a time in the cities and territories. The divine governance of the world is [c] divvied out among the dead saints. [d] The holy angels are worshiped. God's honor [e] is ascribed, in [f] her songs, to the saints, especially to the Virgin Mary. The saints are called upon [g] as her helpers in every need. Their relics (although [h] a great deception has been promulgated as to their true origin) are afforded [i] spiritual honor. The honor that belongs to God alone [j] is

given to images, most notably [k] the image of the crucifix. The [l] bread of the Supper is worshiped as if it were Christ Himself. Oaths are administered [m] not only in God's name, but also [n] in the name of the saints. All of this is an affront to godly piety.

(a) Platina in vita Steph. 3. pag. 118. 1. (b) Extravag. comm. lib. 5. tit. 10. de sent. Excom. c. 2. provide. (c) Zwing. Theat. p. 1405. etc. (d) Staplet. Prompt. Cath. Festo Mich. §. unie. (e) Hack. 2. Frag. Cap. 36. p. 507. (f) ib. p. 503. seq. (g) Himmel. de Invocat. part. 2. Class. 3. c. 1. p. 247. seq. (h) Hospin. de orig. Templ. c. 7. p. 125. (i) Bellar. lib. 2. de reliq. cap. 1. seq. (j) Bellarm. lib. 2. de Imag. cap. 21. seq. Bejerl. Conc. select. 21. pag. 407. seq. (k) Bellar. lib. 2. de Imag. cap. 26. seq. Pontificale fol. 185. fac. 3. (l) Pontificale fol. 197. fac. 3. Bellarmin. lib. 4. de Euchar. cap. 29. (m) Deu. 6:13. (n) Caus. 12. quaest. 5. cap. 16. honestum. caus. 35. quaest. 6. cap. 5. de Parentela.

[19] With regard to the Second Table, the Fourth Commandment is greatly weakened [a] through monastic life. The Fifth, [b] by fasting, self-flagellation, etc. The Sixth, by [c] the prohibition of marriage to those in the spiritual estate. The Seventh, by [d] greed and by [e] the cords of covetousness with which the priests draw the goods of the world to themselves. The Eighth, by [f] the interpretation of an oath according to the understanding of the one who performs it. The Ninth and Tenth, when it is taught [g] that evil thoughts do not pollute a person's mind, as long as he doesn't think them willingly.

(a) caus. 20. quaest. 2. cap. 1. Si in qualibet. (b) Isa. 58:5; Col. 2:16,21; 1 Kings 18:28. (c) caus. 32. quaest. 8. cap. 1. non solum. (d) dist. 93. cap. 23. Diaconi sunt. (e) caus. 13. quaest. 2. cap. 7. placuit per omnia. cap. 8 si quis irascitur. (f) caus. 22. quaest. 5. c. 11. humanae. (g) caus. 33. quaest. 3. dist. 2. cap. 23. inter haec.

[20] (VI) The Roman Church plunges Christians back into Judaism, heathenism, and heresy. The Roman Church has not remained steadfast in apostolic purity, but has strayed miserably from it.

(1) She has adopted [a] heathen practices, [b] laws, ordinances, and [c] a good deal of heathen worship, as she has blended various

aspects of heathenism into Christianity, such as [d] the unchristian punishment of the interdict, [e] the wealth of the clergy, [f] purgatory, in short, all the statuary, veneration of the saints, vows, pilgrimages, seasons, processions, miracles, and many other aspects of heathen worship, as is obvious.

(a) Baron. anno 44. §. 86. seq. (b) ibid. anno 226. §. 5. (c) Polyd. Verg. lib. 4. de Invent. cap. 14. p. 380 lib. 5. cap. 1. p. 381. (d) ibid. lib. 4. cap. 12. pag. 360. Zwinger. Theatr. pag. 821. a. (e) Baron. anno 324. §. 117. seq. (f) Bellar. lib. 1. de purg. cap. 11. §. tertia ratio. Bejerl. conc. select. 25. p. 525. seq.

[21] (2) She has adopted [a] the ways and practices of the Jewish laws. She has [b] her traditions from the Jews, as also [c] the dignity of the high priest, that is, the pope, [d] the division of the ecclesiastical offices, [e] monastic orders, [f] the death penalty for heretics, [g] holy water, [h] altar, holy orders, feast days, fasts, etc.

(a) Baron. anno 18. §. 1. (b) Becan. Man. lib. 1. c. 2. §. 2. seq. 3. §. 10. (c) Bellar. l. 1. de Rom. Pontif. c. 9. (d) dist. 21. part. 1. Polyd. Verg. lib. 4. de Invent. cap. 12. pag. 352. (e) Baron. anno 64. §. 4. seq. Polyd. Verg. lib. 7. cap. 10. pag. 560. (f) Bellarm. lib. 3. de Laic. cap. 21. (g) Anton. Marsil. Column. hydrag. sect. 2. cap. 2. §. 30. seq. (h) Bellarm. lib. 3. de cultu Sanct. cap. 5. §. secunda proposition. §. deinde in statu.

[22] (3) She has made herself a participant with heretics, for the Roman Church has become a refuge for them. [a] Priscillian found refuge there, as did the heresy of the Gnostics. There [b] the Manichaeans held their public meetings, etc. As a result of these interactions, the Roman Church received Communion under only one kind [c] from the Manichaeans, [d] the forbidding of marriage and foods from the Tatians and Encratites, [e] the fasting seasons from the Montanists, the supposed [f] purity of the clergy from Jovinian. Nor can it be ignored that all these things are unmistakable harbingers of the impending ruin of the Roman Church, who must soon return to the heathen, Jews, and heretics all that she once received from them.

(a) Baron. anno 381. §. 109. (b) Bar. anno 372. §. 112. seq. (c) Jacob Hack. wider Tossan. 2. Frag. cap. 45. p. 673. (d) Caus. 24. quaest. 3. c. 39. quidam autem. Platina in vita Pii I. p. 21. a. (e) Hack. 2. Frag 1. cap. 40. p. 547. (f) Caus. 33. q. 3. dist. 2. c. 40. si enim, inquit.

[23] (VII) The Roman Church has robbed Christians of all comfort in life and in death. For she is not willing [a] that anyone should know for certain that he stands in God's grace. No one [b] should be sure of the Holy Spirit's testimony and comfort. No one [c] should believe with certainly that he received a valid Baptism, nor [d] that he has truly received any Sacrament at all. No one should be certain [e] that God has called him to His kingdom, [f] forgiven him his sins, and [g] justified him in His courtroom. No one should be certain [h] that he has truly been converted to God, [i] truly repented, or [j] attained the true, saving faith. Therefore, no one can also be certain [k] whether he will enjoy eternal salvation. But where this foundation has been laid, there no letter of indulgence, no Mass, no merits or intercessions of the saints, etc., can still or console an afflicted, troubled conscience. Instead, [l] one is left to mourn, like the rest who have no hope.

(a) Bellarm. lib. 3. de justif. cap. 11. §. respondeo, posset. Greg. de Valent. Tom. 2. disp. 8. quaest. 4. punct. 4. pag. 1257. a. (b) Becanus tem. 1. Opusc. de justific. Calv. cap. 11. pag. 255. de justific. Cathol. cap. 8. pag. 274. (c) Colloq. Ratispon. Sess. 12. pag. 279. 280 edit. Monach. (d) Bellarm. lib. 3. de justific. cap. 8. §. dicent fortasse. cap. 11. §. itaque non sunt. (e) Bellarm. lib. 3. de justific. c. 13. Greg. de Val. Tom. 1. Quaest. 13. punct. 6. p. 532. (f) Bellarm. lib. 3. de justific. c. 3. §. Lovanienses. Greg. de Valent. Tom. 2. dis. 8. quaest. 4. punct. 4. pag. 1253. d. pag. 1267. a. seq. (g) Concil. Trident. sess. 6. cap. 9. Bellarm. & Greg. de Valent. l. d. (h) Gregor. de Valent. Tom. 2. disp. 8. quaest. 4. punct. 4. pag. 1265. b. seq. pag. 1267. b. pag. 1283. b. c. (i) Greg. de Valent. l. d. pag. 1266. seq. (j) Bellarm. lib. 1. de justific. cap. 10. §. deinde peccant. cap. 12. §. Quid? quod ipsi. Becan. Manual. l. 1. cap. 16. quaest. 5. §. 2. (k) Becan. Man. lib. 1. cap. 16. §. 16. (l) 1 The. 4:13.

[24] (VIII) The Roman Church deprives Christians of their

Christian freedom, forcing them into hard servitude. For whoever is subject to her (1) is not allowed to read the Holy Scriptures (as mentioned [a] earlier) and thus is forced to wander about [b] in the darkness, which is a terrible form of servitude. (2) The laity—all who are not priests—are not permitted to learn [c] the secrets of the Church, or to know much else [d] concerning the Ten Commandments, the articles of the Creed, or Baptism. They must be satisfied [e] with a dark and murky faith. For this reason, the Divine Service is also held in [f] an unknown language. (3) They are supposed [g] to trust the pope blindly and fully, never contradicting him, [h] even if he should lead many thousands of souls into hell. They must [i] bear his yoke, even though it is nearly unbearable. Nor are they allowed [j] to judge whether the doctrine of their teachers is correct or incorrect. (4) They [k] may not read the writings of "heretics" (that is, any who disagree with the Roman Church). (5) Much less are they permitted [l] to discuss matters of faith, [m] especially with "heretics." All this [n] was free in the Apostolic Church; it is the Roman Church that has introduced all such rules and prohibitions.

(a) num. 2. (b) Psa. 119:105. (c) 5 decretal. tit. 7. de haereticis, cap. 12. cum ex injuncto. (d) Gretser. defens. 1. lib. 4. cap. 11. pag. 1797. c. p. 1801. c. pag. 1802. b. (e) ibid. pag. 1799. b. seq. (f) Lancell. haeret. quare 20. (g) Hosius lib. 3. de aut. Script. p. 574. a. (h) dist. 40. cap. 6. Si Papa. (i) dist. 19. cap. 3. In memoriam. (j) dist. 21. c. 6. denique. Caus. 33. quaest. 3. dist. 6. cap. 1. qui vult. Stapleton. Promp. Cathol. Domin. 6. post Epiph. §. 1 pag. 68. (k) Lancell. haer. quare 97. Bejerl. Conc. select. 13. (l) Sext. lib. 5. tit. 2. de haer. cap. 2. qucunque. (m) Bejerl. Conc. select. 12. (n) Mat. 7:15 ff.; 1 John 4:1; John 10:5; Acts 11:1; 1 Cor. 10:15; 1 The. 5:20.

[25] (IX) The Roman Church accomplishes everything in the Church through hypocrisy. (1) The pope [a] calls himself a servant of all Christ's servants. Yet he exalts himself [b] above the highest heights of the world, so that [c] the emperor must seek the pope's permission to appoint a stableman. (2) The clergy [d] hold other people

in contempt, [e] as if they were so filled with the Holy Spirit's grace that nothing could be added to it, while others [f] can hardly pray for themselves, much less for others. (3) People are [g] only to receive the Holy Supper on an empty stomach, and [h] afterwards they are to fast for a few hours. But at the celebration of the Mass, [i] no woman is to approach the altar. It [j] has already been shown above how this Holy Sacrament is dishonored. (4) Prayers [k] are supposed to be more powerful when offered in the church than in other places. They are also [l] just as good and effective, [m] even if a person does not understand them, as long as they are uttered with many words. (5) Fasting is supposed to be [n] a form of worship, even though [o] it cannot make anyone acceptable before God. One is supposed to [p] refrain from eating meat, and yet he can fill up on [q] wine and other foods. (6) In the confession of sins, one should [r] consider things that are not sins to be sins. (7) There are innumerable examples of hypocrisy that could be added to these: [s] Monks are not allowed to have their own property, and yet [t] they can live in luxury. The clergy [u] are not supposed to spill blood, and yet they do. Husbands [v] are not permitted to hold church office, but [w] unchaste people are allowed to hold Mass on a daily basis. In addition, the Roman Church also [x] persecutes most terribly the confessors of the Lord Jesus (who speak out against the public abominations of the Roman Church), under the pretense that she is seeking to protect God's honor, and yet [y] she has no problem allowing the Lord Jesus and the entire Christian religion to be even more terribly blasphemed by the Jews in their synagogues.

(a) 1. decretal. tit. 33. de majorit. & obed. cap. 6. solicitae. (b) ibid. (c) dist. 96. cap. 14. Constantinus. Gretser. defens. 2. Append. ad lib. 3. pag. 1002. b. c. (d) caus. 10. quaest. 1. cap. 15. hanc consuetudinem. (e) caus. 6. quaest. 1. cap. 7. Si omnia. (f) Caus. 10. q. 1. cap. 15. hanc consuetudinem. (g) caus. 7. quaest. 1. cap. 16. nihil contra. (h) de consecrat. dist. 2. cap. 23. tribus. (i) 3. decretal. tit. 2. de cohabit. Cler. cap. 1. Inhibendum. (j) num. 15. (k) Bejerl. Conc. select. 40. pag. 745. (l)

Staplet. Promt. Cathol. Dom. Palm. §. 2. p. 124. Bejerl. Conc. select. 19. p. 367. (m) Bzov. an. 1204. §. 11. Lancell. haeret. quare 22. (n) Staplet. Promt. Cathol. Dom. infra oct. Nativ. §. 2. (o) Hosius. lib. 4. de tradit. p. 632. b. (p) Bellar. lib. 2. de bon. oper. in partic. cap. 5. (q) Bellar. ibid. §. sed objicit: et seq. (r) 5. decret. tit. 12. de homicid. cap. 17. Petrus. de consecrate. dist. 1. c. 41. in sancta. & cap. seq. (s) 3. decret. tit. 35. de statu Monach. cap. 2. Monachi. (t) Caus. 12. quaest. 2. c. 75. Religiosam. (u) Caus. 23. quaest. 7. praefat. cap. 7. Igitur. vide capp. seqq. (v) dist. 28. cap. 2. decernimus. (w) Innocent. 3. lib. 2. de contemtu mundi. cap. 22. (x) Bejerl. Conc. select. 18. (y) 5. decret. tit. 6. de Judaeis, &c. cap. 3. Judaei. c. 7. consuluit.

[26] (X) The Roman Church binds all Christians to such a head as cannot be the head of Christians, namely, [a] to the pope, (1) who is the Antichrist and the great enemy of the Lord Christ. (This will be treated in the last main point.) (2) It is unknown to all of Christendom whether a given pope is truly the pope. For he who is [b] not legitimately chosen, who has [c] gone astray from the faith (although secretly) and has become a heretic, or who has forfeited the office [d] by mismanagement of it or [e] by a wicked life is not truly the pope. But since no one in the world can know this, so also no one knows if the one who is supposed to be the pope really is the pope. (3) The pope is [f] too small to perform his office. He [g] ordains as salutary that which is actually harmful, thus [h] putting souls in danger. Instead of [i] deciding cases himself, even the decree not to marry, he [j] entrusts the judgment to the whim of others. He has [k] never been able to understand and still to this day cannot risk making a determination on that old controversy about whether the Virgin Mary was conceived and born in original sin. Nor is he able [l] to impart to Christians the spiritual power of faith and love. And yet a head must certainly do these things.

(a) Extr. com. lib. 1. tit. 8. de Major. & obed. c. 1. unam sanct. (b) dist. 63. c. 31. inter nos. Caus. 3. q. 1. c. 6. Deus ergo. (c) dist. 40. c. 6. Si Papa. (d) dist. 81. c. 6. Maximianus. Caus. 1. q. 3. c. 2. si quis dator. (e) Caus. 24. q. 3. c. 7. cum aliquis. Caus. 33. q. 3. dist. 1. c. 70. Ecclesia. (f)

5. decr. tit. 20. de crim. falsi c. 5. licet ad regim. (g) Extrav. Joh. 22. tit. 14. de Verb. sig. c. 3. ad conditorem. (h) Extr. Joh. 22. tit. 9. de Torn. c. 1. quia in futurum. (i) 3. decret. tit. 30. de decim. c. 18. cum sint. (j) Caus. 33. q. 3. dist. 1. cap. 89. quamvis plenitude. (k) Extrav. com. lib. 3. tit. 22. de. rel. & vener. c. 2. grave nimis. trid. Conc. sess. 5. de pecc. orig. (l) Bell. l. 3. de Eccl. mil. c. 5. §. respondeo, neminem posse.

[27] I wanted to explain this to you briefly, dear reader—the immeasurable abomination of the desolation that fills the Roman Church—in order to provide you with a warning, that you may not allow yourself to be seduced by the glory of the papacy, which shines so brightly before the world, and thus plunge headlong with it into the utmost torment of souls; and that you may not be deceived by the flatterers who conceal the abominations, where they can, and seek to depict for you a papacy that has never existed in the world, nor will it ever exist. Test everything diligently and hold onto the good! To that end, and from the heart, I wish you the grace of the Holy Spirit.

[28] In opposition to the things I have written, an unknown author has adduced four proofs that the Roman Church is undoubtedly the true Church.

[29] (I) The Roman Church alone has spread out into all the world, according to the prophecy of Psalm 19.

[30] Answer:

1. This prophecy [a] was already fulfilled by the apostles. Moreover, it has been sufficiently prophesied [b] that the Christian Church will not always spread out so widely.

2. It is not written in the Scriptures that the largest mass of people is always the true Christian Church, for otherwise [c] the weeds must become wheat and [d] the Antichrist, with [e] his false prophets, must be the Church of Christ.

3. In addition, the Roman Church does not stretch through-

out the whole world, for it is not found in Turkey, etc., and in many other kingdoms and countries. Before [f] the Indies were discovered, the Roman Church existed in only one part of the smallest continent. Indeed, the Jesuits contend [g] that the Gospel has not yet been preached in all the world. How is it, then, that the Roman Church extends over all the world without the preaching of the Gospel?

(a) Rom. 10:18; Col. 1:6,23. (b) Mat. 24:24; Luke 18:8; Rev. 12:6. (c) Mat. 13:19. (d) Rev. 13:3,4,7; Rev. 17:2. (e) Mat. 24:24. (f) Gretser. defens. 2. lib. 3. cap. 4. p. 855. d. (g) Bellarm. lib. 3. de Rom. Pontif. cap. 4. Grets. defens. ejusd. Tanner. part. 3. Theol. Scholast. disp. 1. quaest. 3. dub. 5.

[31] (II) In Matthew 16:18, St. Peter was made the foundation of the Church, on which the Roman Church was built and now continues through papal succession.

[32] Answer:

1. The rock on which the Christian Church is built is [a] not Peter, but Christ.

2. St. Peter never became the head of the Christian Church, for [b] Christ made all the apostles equal. St. Peter [c] never presented himself as a pope, nor did the apostles [d] ever recognize him as such, nor did they direct anyone to him.

3. But even if St. Peter became the head of the Church, how does this help the Roman pope? He cannot claim any succession from St. Peter, for he [e] does not succeed him in doctrine. Indeed, one must include all those popes from the papal registry who (as [f] demonstrated above) were not truly popes, as well as all those who wanted to be the Roman Bishop in [g] times of schism. According to this list, not even a third of the popes would remain. But what kind of succession is that?

(a) dist. 19. cap. 7. ita Dominus. gloss. & super hanc petram. (b) dist. 21. cap. 2. in novo. Caus. 24. quaest. 1. cap. 18. loquitur. (c) Greg. de Valent. Analys. lib. 7. cap. 6. §. haec ita ordina. §. quod autem. (d) 2.

Cor. 11:5; 2 Cor. 12:11; Gal. 2:9. (e) supra num. 20. seq. (f) num. 26. (g) dist. 79. cap. 8. si duo forte.

[33] (III) While all the churches in Jerusalem, Antioch, etc., have fallen, the Roman Church alone has remained steadfast.

[34] Answer:

1. She has fallen spiritually (see [a] above), much more horribly than all the others.

2. But although she has remained outwardly, as [b] the Jewish Church also does, even so [c] she makes her followers into children of hell, [d] just as the Jewish Church does. What kind of Christian Church is that?

(a) num. 20. sq. (b) Mat. 23:2. (c) Rev. 19:20. (d) Mat. 23:13, 15.

[35] (IV) Luther himself testified that God has especially favored the Roman Church and that all these things have remained therein: the Holy Scriptures, the Sacraments, the authority to forgive sins, the preaching office, the catechism—yes, the true Christian Church.

[36] Answer:

1. At one time, God looked with special favor [a] on Chorazin, Bethsaida, and Capernaum. But they were not on that account the true Church. On the contrary, their judgment was that much more severe because of it.

2. [b] The Holy Scriptures, [c] the teachers, [d] the adoption, the glory, the covenant, the Law, the Divine Service, the Promise, the Fathers—yes, Christ Himself and [e] the finest of the godly, pious believers were found in the Jewish Church. But in the end, she [f] shut the gates of heaven [g] with Pharisaical leaven and [h] was rejected as not being God's people. This is the state in which the Roman Church similarly finds herself.

(a) Mat. 11:21 ff. (b) Rom. 3:2. (c) Mat. 23:2. (d) Rom. 9:4; Eph. 2:12.

(e) Luke 1:5, 6, 27; Luke 2:25,37,38. (f) Mat. 23:13. (g) Mat. 16:12. (h) Hosea 1:9; Rom. 11:20.

The Second Chief Point.

The Most Precious Sacrament of the Altar.

The first question: Is it sufficient for a Christian's salvation to receive the most precious Sacrament of the Altar under only one kind?

[37] No. For the one who wishes to benefit from the Supper, one kind is insufficient.

[38] (I) Because the Roman Church herself does not believe that it is enough for a priest to hold the Mass in only one kind, even though he receives as much in the one kind as in both. How, then, should it be enough for the laity, since they both have a single institution?

[39] (II) Because he who receives only one kind rescinds half of Christ's institution. Christ instituted [a] two kinds—the bread and the wine—so that all who participate in this Communion should be offered all that pertains to the substance of the Sacrament. Therefore, they [b] must both eat and drink. Since the Lord uses the imperatives, "Eat," and, "Drink," and could not have expressed the command more clearly, His Church is thus bound to this ordinance and has [c] no power to do anything to the contrary.

(a) Clement. lib. 3. tit. 16. de Reliq. cap. un. si Dominum. Concil. Constant. sess. 13. Tom. 2. Concil. p. 1068. b. Concil. Trid. sess. 21. cap. 2. (b) Mat. 26:26,27. (c) Hack. 2. Frag. Cap. 45. pag. 680.

[40] And although the words, [a] "Drink of it, all of you," in the first institution were spoken only to the apostles, they were there as communicants (and as representatives of the entire Christian Church) and not as priests (since they were not holding any kind of Mass there). Otherwise, the entire Supper would be ordained only for the priests, and the laity would have no part in it whatsoever.

(a) Mat. 26:27.

[41] (III) Because the Sacrament, which is incomplete without the cup, is torn apart and mutilated. The above-mentioned institution demonstrates this clearly, as it gives command [a] as strongly about the cup as it does about the bread. Indeed, [b] the pope himself explains this, that without the cup, Communion is not complete, but is mutilated. And whoever does not receive the cup does so out of unbelief and thereby commits sacrilege.

(a) Mat. 26:26,27. (b) Consecr. dist. 2. cap. 12. comperimus.

[42] (IV) Because it changes the necessary custom of the Christian Church. Both kinds were offered [a] in the Apostolic Church, which then became common [b] in the ancient Church, as [c] the writings of the ancient Church Fathers testify. [d] The schoolmasters, too, argued vigorously against it, and [e] Pope Julius rebuked much abuse among the laity which had to do with receiving the cup. Indeed, [f] no one knows when Communion in one kind began, since it crept in little by little, together [g] with other abuses, ever since [h] the Manichaeans first introduced it in Rome, although they were rebuked for it. Indeed, it is beyond controversy that the Roman Church, prior to [i] the Council at Basel (200 years ago), had made no rulings about this, but simply allowed the practice to continue where the people themselves wanted it to continue.

(a) 1 Cor. 10:16,21; 1 Cor. 11:26 ff. (b) de consec. dist. 2. cp. 37. cum frangitur. Bejerl. Conc. select. 32. pag. 610. (c) vide D. Gerh. Tom. 6. de Coena, cap. 9. §. 43. Phil. Morn. Pless. de Euchar. lib. 1. c. 10. (d) Lombard. lib. 4. sent. dist. 11. F. Ales. part. 4. quaest. 32. mem. 1. art. 2. &c. (e) de consecr. dist. 2. cap. 7. cum omne. (f) Hosius de comm. utr. spec. p. 718. a. (g) de cons. dist. 2. c. 7. cum omne. (h) Bellar. lib. 4. de Euch. c. 24. §. quarta ratio. Hack. 2. Frage. Cap. 45. pag. 673. (i) Conc. Trident. sess. 21. cap. 2.

[43] (V) Because there is no solid basis for Communion under one kind on which the conscience can rest secure.

The following arguments are offered as a solid basis for Communion under one kind:

[44] (1) A person receives under one kind as much as he receives under both; namely, both the body and the blood of Christ.

[45] Answer:

1. There is no Word of God that addresses this. But if one wishes to place the matter in the realm of speculation, then the entire Sacrament must fall.

2. Christ did not teach us to receive His blood under the bread, nor His body under the wine, nor did He promise to give them to us in this way, nor did He command us, "Eat. This is My body and blood, etc." Therefore, even if as much were received in one form as in two, nevertheless we must observe the institution of Christ, which commands us to use both kinds.

3. According to this notion, there is no reason why the entire Mass should not also be performed under only one kind.

4. Indeed, the celebrant at the Mass who receives the Sacrament in both kinds would be receiving the same thing twice!

5. But the Roman Church can by no means prove that the body and blood of Christ are both received in only one kind. Therefore, it remains a human notion.

[46] (2) From this statement: "Christ would then be divided, which is an Antichristian dogma."

Answer:

1. The Holy Sacrament is a mystery in which we allow Christ to dictate the manner in which He arranges His own ordinance. That alone is what we are to observe.

2. The institution of Christ divides the body and blood of the Lord in such a way that both are promised in bread and wine,

but separately. We must also allow this to stand.

3. However, the Roman Church divides bread and cup (and thus the body and blood of Christ), which Christ does not wish to be divided. She mixes into one kind that which Christ divided into two. Is that Christian or Antichristian?

[47] (3) From the sixth chapter of John, where man's salvation is attributed several times to the bread.

Answer:

1. John 6 is not dealing with the Holy Sacrament (which was instituted almost a year later), since the Sacrament [a] can be received for judgment (but not [b] the bread of which John 6 speaks). And a person can be saved without the Sacrament (but not [c] without the bread of which John 6 speaks).

2. John 6 does not refer to a sacramental eating and drinking, but to a spiritual eating and drinking, which is [d] equivalent to believing, in which case, eating and drinking are a single thing.

3. Even if Christ had said nothing whatsoever about drinking in John 6, it would still be enough that He gave a clear command about it at the institution of the Sacrament, [e] "Drink of it, all of you." Furthermore, the entire meal (in John 6) would have been understood through the bread, [f] which is a common manner of speaking.

4. The drinking of the blood of Christ is also commanded and abundantly commended in John 6: [g] "If you do not drink My blood, then you have no life in you. [h] Whoever drinks My blood has eternal life. [i] My blood is the true drink. [j] Whoever drinks My blood remains in Me, and I in him."

(a) 1 Cor. 11:29. (b) 1 Cor. 11:51, 56. (c) 1 Cor. 11:53. (d) 1 Cor. 11:35,37. (e) Mat. 26:27. (f) Luke 14:1, etc. (g) 1 Cor. 11:53. (h) 1 Cor. 11:54. (i) 1 Cor. 11:55. (j) 1 Cor. 11:56.

[48] (4) There were shadows and types of it in the Scripture: The tree of life, the Passover lamb, the manna, the showbread, the feeding of the 5,000 with five loaves of bread. In none of these was there any drink.

[49] Answer:

1. The types prove nothing unless the thing itself already has a solid basis.

2. Even if all the types excluded the drinking, Christ's instruction commanding it would still take precedence.

3. But assuming that all these were types of the Holy Supper, it certainly follows that one must use both kinds: [a] There was drinking along with the Passover lamb. They certainly must have drunk [b] along with the manna. It cannot be proved that the showbread had to be eaten without drink, or that there was no drink [c] with the tree of life.

4. And if the types apply that widely, then the Christian Church should not allow the drinking of the Supper either to priests or to laymen, especially since [d] the Nazarites were not allowed to drink wine during their entire life, while [e] the priests could not drink it when they were attending to the divine service.

5. Indeed, one would have to use only the cup during the Mass, since the rock (which was [f] a picture of Christ) gave [g] only drink, not food. And the Israelites were [h] merely sprinkled with the blood of the Levitical Testament; the flesh was not distributed to them. These (not to mention others) are more certain types than those cited by Rome.

(a) Luke 22:17. (b) Exo. 17:1 ff; Num. 20:2 ff. (c) Gen. 2:9,10. (d) Num. 6:3. (e) Lev. 10:9. (f) 1 Cor. 10:4. (g) Num. 20:11. (h) Exo. 24:5, 8.

[50] (5) A misinterpretation of the Lord's Prayer: Christ did not teach us to ask for wine, but bread. And the Canaanite woman

only asked for bread crumbs from the Lord's table.

[51] Answer:

1. All Christians ask in the Fourth Petition, not for the Holy Supper (which belongs in the Second Petition), but [a] for bodily nourishment.

2. Even if this were true, the priests would then have to be happy with bread in the Mass, or they would have to make up their own Our Father.

3. Nor could the Christian Church ever again allow anyone to drink the cup, or else the Our Father would have to be changed.

4. The Canaanite woman at that time did not ask for the bread of the Supper, but, in figurative speech, [b] for a work of the miraculous grace of Christ.

5. Something else follows from this: the laity, for the same reason, should only receive the cup, since [c] the Samaritan woman only asked for the water of life, not for bread, and the Lord only promised her water.

6. But Christ's institution makes all such thoughts irrelevant.

(a) Emser Gloss über Mat. 6. (b) Mat. 15:22, 26, 27. (c) John 4:10, 15.

[52] (6) Absurd examples: At [a] Emmaus, in [b] the apostolic churches, and in the times following, the Supper was offered under only one kind.

(a) Luke 24:30. (b) Acts 2:46; Acts 20:7.

[53] Answer:

1. The papists [a] are uncertain whether the Supper was held at Emmaus (some of them [b] expressly deny that it was).

2. It would follow that Christ must have held Mass without wine and in only one kind.

3. And since the two disciples were priests, the priests must have only received one kind.

4. But there is neither proof nor indication that the Holy Supper was actually celebrated there.

5. Since [c] the practice of the Lord Christ was to break bread and hand it out, after giving thanks, He was known by the two disciples (who were not present at the institution of the Supper and had probably heard nothing about it).

(a) Bellar. lib. 4. de Euchar. cap. 24. §. rursus exemplo. (b) Jansen. harmon. cap. 146. (c) Mat. 14:19; John 6:11.

[54] In the apostolic churches:

1. [a] The cup was not excluded. Even though [b] mention is only made of the bread, it is common knowledge that [c] bread signifies a whole meal, and whoever invites a person to eat with him also invites him to drink.

2. If there had been no wine there, then the apostles would have held Mass without wine.

3. It is clear [d] that both kinds were used in the ancient church, and the unknown writer admits it when [e] he writes: "Thus Alensis, Albertus Magnus, St. Thomas Aquinas, and St. Bonaventura testify that, at their time, it had become the common practice in nearly (note: 'nearly') the whole Church to receive the most precious Sacrament in only one kind."

(a) 1 Cor. 11:25 ff. (b) Acts 2:46; Acts 20:7. (c) Mark 7:2; Luke 14:1. (d) num. 42. (e) pag. 16.

[55] Will a Christian now wonder whether, through Communion under one kind—by which he is nullifying half of the institution of the Lord Jesus, mutilating the Holy Sacrament, and exchanging the necessary Christian usage for something introduced by heretics, and, without reason or cause, abandoning God's Word

for the ideas of men—he forfeits his salvation and receives it for judgment? Indeed, one may also wonder whether it can be the Church of Christ that abuses the Holy Sacrament in this way.

The second question: Why is the freedom to receive the Sacrament in one or both kinds removed, so that only the one kind is permitted?

[56] Answer:

1. Christ's Words do not give the Church the freedom to receive one or two kinds; they bind her to both kinds.

2. The Roman Church has altered this in a most unchristian manner.

3. And that, without a single legitimate reason.

Nevertheless, these are the reasons that are proffered:

[57] (I) Just as one kind was forbidden in times past on account of the Manichaeans, so it is now commanded on account of the Hussites.

[58] Answer: It was right to command both kinds (against the Manichaeans), but only on account of the institution of Christ. But to forbid both kinds in order to spite the Hussites and contrary to Christ's institution is eternally unjustifiable, since [a] no one needs to hear the lie that the command is being kept. Indeed, [b] no one should do evil so that good may result.

(a) Sirach 34:8. (b) Rom. 3:8.

[59] (II) With one kind, there will be greater equality between the healthy and the sick, whether people drink wine or not, whether they live in wine-producing lands or are far removed from them.

[60] Answer:

1. Since the Roman Church is not smarter than Christ, who directly suspended this equality of Christians by means of His

institution, we should and must order ourselves according to this and not according to anyone's whim.

2. But if such equality is supposed to exist, then one must also [a] apply it to the priests, whether they are healthy or sick, whether they are in wine-producing lands or not, etc.

3. Indeed, the bread must be eliminated from the Supper, since the sick can enjoy it even less than the wine.

(a) Bellarm. lib. 4. de Rom. Pontif. 14. §. Quadragesimus.

[61] (III) By offering only one kind, the Antichristian error is mitigated, as if Christ were not entirely alive, but instead were split apart in distinct forms, as if He were dead.

[62] Answer:

1. In that case, let the Roman Church answer to the Lord Christ Himself, since He set it up this way.

2. If that is an Antichristian error, then [a] the Roman Church confirmed it long ago when she commanded both kinds to be used against the Manichaeans.

3. She still confirms it when only the priests are allowed to commune in both kinds.

4. Indeed, since the Christian Church should never introduce a single Antichristian error, she should never again allow both kinds either to priests or to the laity! But [b] this has been addressed above.

(a) Ungenante Scrib. pag. 1617. (b). num. 46.

[63] (IV) One kind has been commanded in order to avoid the great dishonor which would be done to God if the blood of Christ were spilled.

[64] Answer:

1. Christ paid no attention to this when He commanded both kinds. Let us be content with that.

2. It is possible to be careful enough with the cup so that there is no need to be concerned about such a thing.

3. How can we nullify Christ's Testament over such a broad concern?

4. The Roman Church should rather eliminate the bread, which could not only fall to the floor, to God's dishonor, but [a] the Jews could also dishonor it (as often happens). It could also be misused [b] for superstition, murder, witchcraft, etc., for the utmost blasphemy of the Lord Christ. But just as the bread is not taken away on account of these many, terrible abuses, much less should the cup be eliminated on account of a minor, potential abuse.

(a) Baron. Ann. 1306. §. 8. anno 1329. §. 19. 20. (b) num. 15.

[65] (V) Whoever does not wish to be considered a heathen must follow the Christian Church, which has commanded only one kind to be used.

[66] Answer: Even the Christian Church should not be followed if she contradicts Christ's command. The one who follows her in that case is considered a heathen. Therefore, since the Roman Church publicly does this in eliminating the cup, the one who follows her in this case must be considered a heathen.

[67] (VI) Luther himself was of the opinion that a person may properly receive only one kind.

[68] Answer:

1. Even if [a] an angel from heaven should teach this, we should not follow him. So also with Luther. We do not allow ourselves to be bound to him, but only to the Word of God. Therefore, it is not at all necessary to respond to his testimony. It has already been answered a thousand times.

2. Luther taught differently on this point during the first years after his conversion because he was looking out for those who

were weak in faith and could not receive both kinds. Otherwise, he taught zealously and steadfastly against only one kind.

(a) Gal. 1:8.

The Third Main Point.

The Mass.

[69] The Holy Supper was called *Missam* in the old Latin Church, from which the word "Mass" originates. This word, in part, has remained in use in the Evangelical Church.

[70] But when one speaks of the Mass according to the practice of the Roman Church, [a] an atoning sacrifice is understood in which the body and blood of Christ are sacrificed to the heavenly Father. That is, they are given as an offering for the living and the dead.

(a) Concil. Trident. Sess. 22. cap. 2. & Can. 3. Bellarm. lib. 1. de Missa, cap. 5.

[71] There are two things wrong with this: First, through the Mass, the Holy Supper is made into an atoning sacrifice.

[72] (I) There is no basis to be found anywhere for the Mass. All sacrifices have their clear institution. The Mass has none. [a] At the first Supper, Christ did not offer (or sacrifice) His body and blood to the heavenly Father as an offering, nor did He command His disciples to make such a sacrifice. He enjoins them only to eat and to drink in His remembrance.

(a) 1 Cor. 11:24, 25.

[73] (II) The Mass alters the ordinance of Christ. (1) The Lord Jesus ordained a Sacrament in which He offers the communicants His body to eat and His blood to drink. But the Mass turns this into a sacrifice in which the body and blood of Christ are given as an offering. (2) Christ instituted the Holy Supper [a] for all. But the Mass is distributed [b] only to the priests.

(a) 1 Cor. 10:16, 17; 1 Cor. 11:26 ff. (b) Bellarm. lib. 1. de Missa, cap. 17.

[74] (III) The Mass directly opposes the sacrifice of the Lord Christ on the cross. For (1) there is [a] only one Priest who is recognized in the New Testament, only one sacrifice that was performed, and that, only once (without any repetition). [b] It was not necessary for our High Priest to make a sacrifice for sin on a daily basis, for He did it once for all when He sacrificed Himself. [c] Christ entered into the Holy Place once, through His own blood, and founded an eternal redemption. [d] Christ was sacrificed once for all to take away the sins of many. [e] In Christ we have been sanctified, which happened once, through the sacrifice of the body of Jesus Christ. [f] This One made only one sacrifice for sin, which is eternally valid. [g] With one sacrifice He has perfected forever those who are sanctified. [h] Christ entered the Holy Place, not to sacrifice Himself many times, as the high priest enters the Holy Place every year with the blood of another, or else He would have had to suffer many times from the beginning of the world until now. But now, at the end of the world, He has appeared once to remove sin through His own sacrifice. [i] Christ was offered once to take away the ins of many. [j] When Christ died, He died to sin once.

(a) Heb. 7:3, 26. (b) Heb. 7:27. (c) Heb. 9:12. (d) Heb. 9:28. (e) Heb. 10:10. (f) Heb. 10:12. (g) Heb. 10:14. (h) Heb. 9:24 ff. (i) Heb. 9:28. (j) Rom. 6:10.

[75] (2) Christ [a] has performed a perfect sacrifice. But if it is supposed to be repeated in the Mass, then it is thereby interpreted to be just as imperfect as the Levitical sacrifices were, which had to be repeated for that very reason, as [b] the above testimonies demonstrate.

(a) John 1:29; Rom. 8:1. (b) num. 74.

[76] Indeed, it would be truly imperfect, since Christ could not have achieved the atonement with His sacrifice on the cross, if it must first be earned through the sacrifice of the Mass. Why? Because [a] "where there is forgiveness of sins, there is no more sacrifice for sin."

(a) Heb. 10:10.

[77] (IV) If the Mass sheds no blood (for it is supposed to be an unbloody sacrifice), how can it take away sin? For [a] "without the shedding of blood there is no forgiveness."

(a) Heb. 9:22.

[78] (V) The Mass [a] is supposed to represent Christ's sacrifice on the cross, thus bringing back the Old Testament, [b] which was set aside because it was only a mere shadow and representation.

(a) Conc. Trident. sess. 22. c. 2. (b) Col. 2:16, 17; Heb. 10:1.

[79] (VI) There is no evidence in the apostolic and ancient Church that the body and blood of Christ were at that time sacrificed to God as an offering. Therefore, it is also impossible to prove that anyone knew the slightest thing about the Mass in the apostolic and ancient Church.

[80] Nor do the following passages serve to prove that the Mass was celebrated:

(1) In Acts 13:2 it is written: "The teachers at Antioch ministered to God." For the Greek word (λειτουργία) [a] refers to all kinds of service, even in the secular and domestic estates. Thus the Roman Church is also [b] not agreed on that passage, whether she should understand the Mass or some other divine service. Nor can any account about the Mass be given in these words.

(a) Rom. 13:6; Rom. 15:27; 2 Cor. 9:12; Phi. 2:30. (b) Lorinus, Comment. in h. locum. Dietenb. und Emser h. l.

[81] (2) "1 Corinthians 10:16: In Corinth, the cup was blessed." But from that fact it cannot be established that any Mass or sacrifice was offered, which is the question at hand. [a] They offered neither the bread nor the cup to God, but to the communicants.

(a) 1 Cor. 10:16; 1 Cor. 11:26 ff.

[82] (3) "Hebrews 13:10: Christians have an altar, and, therefore, also a sacrifice." This is true. However, the sacrifices are spiri-

tual (as is also the altar), [a] a broken and contrite heart, [b] a reasonable worship, [c] a true faith, [d] praise and thanksgiving, [e] alms, etc., for which no sacrifice of the Mass is needed.

(a) Psa. 51:19. (b) Rom. 12:12. (c) Phi. 2:17. (d) Heb. 13:15. (e) Phi. 4:18.

[83] (4) "The Mass was prefigured in the Old Testament by the everlasting daily sacrifices (Dan. 11:31) and by the clean offering of incense and food which was to be brought to God in every place (Mal. 1:11)." There is no doubt [a] that Christ's sacrifice was prefigured by these things, as were also [b] the other spiritual sacrifices. But how does anyone know that the Mass was intended to be prefigured by these things? Indeed, the Mass would then have to be not just a food offering, but also an incense offering.

(a) Col. 2:17; Heb. 10:1. (b) Hosea 14:3; Psa. 51:21.

[84] (5) "It was the devil who drove Luther to attack the Mass." Even if this were true, it still does make the Mass valid, since it so directly opposes the divine Word. But here is what actually happened: The devil tried to drive Luther to doubt. Since the devil had propagated idolatry with the Mass, and since Luther saw that the Mass could not help at all in times of trial against the devil's attacks, as he himself had experienced in dealing with his own conscience, he sought in God's Word a firm foundation (not at the devil's urging). See [a] Luther's own account.

(a) Im 6. Jen. Theil am. 82. 83. Blat.

The Fourth Chief Point.

The Invocation and Intercession of the Saints.

[85] There is no doubt among Christians that one should honor the saints who have died, as [a] they themselves want to be honored, even as [b] other saints, who died before they did, honored them when they were alive in the world.

(a) Luke 1:48; Luke 11:27. (b) Rom. 4:17 ff.; 1 Pet. 1:10 ff.; Heb. 11:4 ff.

[86] But it is an unchristian thing to honor them with spiritual veneration, as the Roman Church urges. For:

(1) This invocation has no foundation in God's Word. There is no command, no promise that such prayers will be heard; no example, not a single report that such invocation is pleasing to God.

[87] (2) Invocation is an honor that belongs to God, an honor [a] that He is not willing to share with anyone else. Therefore, [b] all the commands regarding invocation, [c] all the promises attached to it, [d] all the formulas and [e] examples have only God in view, so that, [f] where any creature is called upon with spiritual devotion, there idolatry has been committed.

(a) Isa. 42:8. (b) Psa. 50:15; Psa. 91:15. (c) Mat. 7:11; John 16:23. (d) Exo. 15:1; Mat. 6:9. (e) Psa. 18:7; Eph. 3:14. (f) Rom. 1:23, 25.

[88] (3) No Christian may call upon the saints, either as helpers or as intercessors. *Not as helpers.* For whoever asks the saints for benefits of body and soul, on the basis of their merits, considers the merits of the Lord Christ either to be worthless, or at least insufficient and useless for our wellbeing. For [a] "through His sacrifice those who are being sanctified are eternally perfected." Instead, he

sets another name [b] above the name of Christ by which we must be saved. He also attaches human merits, which have been rejected by God and by the saints themselves, to the merits of Christ (yes, he puts them ahead of Christ's merit!), even though human merits [c] are like filthy rags [d] of which one should be ashamed, with which one must appear as [e] an unworthy servant. Consider whether it is a Christian practice to hide the merits of your Redeemer while highlighting the merits of the saints.

(a) Heb. 10:14. (b) Acts 4:12. (c) Isa. 64:6. (d) Dan. 9:7. (e) Luke 17:10.

[89] *Not as intercessors.* For it is true and indisputable that living Christians on earth pray for one another, since [a] they have God's command to do so, as well as [b] divine promises and [c] praiseworthy examples. [d] Noah prayed for the living creatures after the Flood. [e] Abraham prayed for Abimelech. [f] Job prayed for his friends.

(a) Mat. 6:9 ff.; 1 Tim. 2:1, 2. (b) James 5:16. (c) Exo. 32:32; Num. 12:13; 1 Cor. 1:10, 11. (d) Gen. 8:20. (e) Gen. 20:7, 17. (f) Job 42:8.

[90] Moreover, it is certainly true that [a] the saints pray for the general wellbeing of the Christian Church. But that they know anyone's condition and need in particular (apart from what they experienced in life, as [b] the rich man knew the condition of his brethren)—that is expressly contradicted by the Word of God: [c] The dead know nothing. [d] If his children come to honor, he does not know it. Or if they are lowly, he is not aware of it. [e] Abraham does not know of us, and Israel does not recognize us.

Indeed, such knowledge on the part of the dead can never by any means be investigated or proven, not to mention that it is God's special attribute [f] to know the hearts of all the children of men, and [g] to see the prayer that is offered in secret.

(a) Rev. 5:8. (b) Luke 16:27, 28. (c) Ecc. 9:5. (d) Job 14:21. (e) Isa. 63:16. (f) 1 Kings 8:39. (g) Mat. 6:6.

[91] In addition, such prayer runs contrary to the intercessory office of Christ, since there is only [a] one Mediator between God and men, the Man Christ Jesus. It also stands opposed to His office as Advocate, since [b] He sits at the right hand of God and intercedes for us, so that, [c] if anyone sins, we have an Advocate with the Father, Jesus Christ. If this office is truly authoritative and perfect, then it must be idolatrous to ascribe it to the saints.

(a) 1 Tim. 2:5. (b) Rom. 8:34. (c) 1 John 2:1.

[92] (4) The saints do not acknowledge the spiritual worship that is done to them. [a] Peter would not accept such worship from Cornelius, because he was a man. Indeed, even [b] the angel prevented John from worshiping him when John wanted to, saying, "Do not do it! I am your fellow servant and your brother. Worship God!"

(a) Acts 10:25, 26. (b) Rev. 19:10

[93] (5) The invocation of the saints is a truly heathen work, since it was entirely unknown in the ancient Christian Church and has its origin in heathenism. For just as the heathen [a] divided the governing of the world among their gods, assigning to each country, city, house, man, animal, etc., its own patron, [b] and honored their dead by building churches and altars, with fast days, sacrifices and offerings, by exalting their bones, images, seasons, etc., so, too, the Roman Church does—which is truly heathen, but very unchristian.

(a) Natal. Comes, Mythol. lib. 1. c. 10. pag. 34. (b) Idem lib. 4. cap. 2. pag. 294. seq.

The following objections are made:

[94] (1) "Moses [a] prayed to God: Remember Your servants, Abraham, Isaac and Israel, etc."

Answer: Moses reminds God of His [b] promise which He had spoken to the patriarchs concerning their descendants. This is what he says: "Remember Your servants, Abraham, etc., to whom You swore by Yourself and promised, 'I will multiply your seed, as the stars of heaven, and all the land, etc.'" Any reasonable person can easily see that here there is no report either of invocation or of intercession.

(a) Exo. 32:13. (b) Gen. 17:15, 26:4, 28:14.

[95] (2) [a]"With regard to Ephraim and Manasseh, Jacob commanded that his name (and that of Abraham and Isaac) should be invoked upon them."

Answer:

1. The Hebrew text makes it clear that there is no religious veneration or invocation being commanded in this passage, but that Jacob wanted his grandsons to be called by his name, to be considered his children and not Joseph's. It was for this reason, then, that they were always treated as [b] two distinct tribes in Israel.

2. That is what it means to be "called by his name," [c] which is a common way of speaking.

3. No one ever prayed to Abraham on behalf of Ephraim and Manasseh.

4. Therefore, [d] the papists themselves interpret this text as we have demonstrated here, not concerning any invocation or prayers.

(a) Gen. 48:16. (b) Num. 1:33-34; Num. 2:18, 20; Joshua 16:5; Joshua 16:1. (c) Isa. 4:1; Dan. 9:19. (d) Arias Montan. in h. l. Lyra in h. l. Ribera in Amos. 9. num. 42.

The Fifth Chief Point.

Purgatory.

[96] Purgatory is supposed to be [a] a place near hell in which the souls that did not make satisfaction for all their sins in this world must pay for them through the tortures of hell before they are received into the blessedness of heaven.

(a) Bellarm. lib. 1. de Purgat. cap. 1. §. vocatur. Concil. Trid. sess. 6. Can. 30.

[97] But it is proven that there is no such thing as purgatory: (1) No one knew anything about it in the Apostolic Church. It crept in [a] from heathenism and was confirmed [b] by false revelations and even apparitions of Satan.

(a) Bellarm. lib. 1. de Purgat. cap. 11. §. tertia ratio. Bejerl. conc. select. 28. pag. 524. seq. Natal. Comes lib. 3. c. 9. p. 174. cap. 20. pag. 286. Ludov. de la Cerda Comm. in Verg. 6. Aeneid. vers. 609. not. 1. & vers. 735. sq. (b) Bellar. lib. 1. de purgat. c. 11. §. quarta ratio.

[98] (2) God's Word tells us of only [a] two places where souls go—heaven and hell—[b] without anyone having to pass through purgatory first. No third place is ever mentioned.

(a) Luke 16:22-23; Mark 16:16; Mark 9:44; Mat. 25:34, 43. (b) John 5:24.

[99] (3) And although [a] the condition after this life is often addressed—[b] funerals and [c] mourning over the dead, the [d] admonitions for which estates one should pray, and also [e] the sacrifices for all kinds of sins, etc.—still not a single word is said anywhere about purgatory or about those who are supposedly sitting therein. That would be impossible if purgatory really existed.

(a) Wisdom 3:1; Psa. 49:15, 20; Job 10:22 ff. (b) Gen. 23:19; Gen.

35:8,19; Num. 20:1 ff. (c) Gen. 50:10, 11; 1 Kings 13:30. (d) 1 Tim. 2:1. (e) Lev. 4:5 ff.

[100] (4) The condition of believers in this world does not allow for the existence of purgatory. For they [a] have peace with God. They serve God during their whole life [b] without fear. They are [c] joyful in hope. They live as [d] children of God in the kingdom of God, that is, in [e] spiritual peace and joy. They [f] eagerly await the redemption of their body. And they [g] desire to depart, since they know that they will [h] never again thirst. None of this can be true if they must await purgatory.

(a) Rom. 5:1. (b) Luke 1:74. (c) Rom. 12:12. (d) 1 John 3:2. (e) Rom. 14:17. (f) Rom. 8:22, 23. (g) Luke 2:29; Phil 1:23. (h) John 4:14.

[101] (5) The condition of the blessed dead does not allow for it. For they are [a] "justified from sins." They have come [b] to "rest" and [c] "peace." They [d] "rest in the hands of God without any torment." They are [e] "carried to Abraham's bosom" immediately after they die. And, therefore, they are lauded as [f] "blessed from now on." None of this can coexist with purgatory.

(a) Rom. 6:7. (b) Sirach 22:11. (c) Isa. 57:2. (d) Wisdom 3:1. (e) Luke 16:22. (f) Rev. 14:13.

[102] (6) The high priestly office of Christ does not allow for it. He [a] carried all our sins. He not only [b] paid for guilt, but also [c] bore the punishment so that we might have peace. In summary, He [d] washed us by His blood from all uncleanness, so that [e] nothing damning might be found in those who are in Christ Jesus. What, then, is left for the fires of purgatory to purge?

(a) John 1:29; 1 Pet. 2:24. (b) Psa. 69:5. (c) Isa. 53:5. (d) 1 John 1:7; Rev. 1:5. (e) Rom. 8:1.

[103] (7) The application of the merit of Christ does not allow for it. This is what happens through repentance: [a] "If we confess our sins, God is faithful and just to forgive us our sins and to cleanse us from all unrighteousness." Through the Holy Sacraments: [b] "Christ

sanctified His Church and cleansed her through the washing with water in the Word, so that she might be holy and blameless." Through faith: [c]"God cleanses our hearts through faith." And thus the elect [d]"have their robes washed and made clean in the blood of the Lamb." What, then, is the purpose of purgatory?

(a) 1 John 1:9. (b) Eph. 5:26, 27. (c) Acts 15:9. (d) Rev. 7:14.

[104] (8) The examples in Scripture do not allow for it: [a] The criminal who was crucified with Christ; [b] Lazarus; and [c] others who, according to the papistic fantasies, would surely have needed the cleansing of purgatory before they should have come into the heavenly kingdom, and yet they were not sent there. In the same way, [d] God will take to Himself the believers who are alive on the earth on the Last Day without any such purging.

(a) Luke 23:43. (b) Luke 16:22. (c) Rev. 7:13, 14. (d) 1 The. 4:17.

[105] (9) And if there were such a place as purgatory and [a] the pope had full authority to release from it those who are dear to him, then he would, without delay, free all the souls from it (if there were a single drop of Christian blood in his veins). But since he does not do this, he demonstrates either his inhumanity, or that there is no purgatory.

(a) Vide D. Meisneri opusc. sec. de Indulg. cap. 12. scrup. 9. pag. 1200. seq.

In opposition to this, some wish to prove the existence of purgatory with the following arguments:

[106] (1) "Zechariah 9:11: You release Your prisoners, through the blood of the covenant, from the grave, wherein there is no water."

Answer:

1. The Roman Church [a] does not attempt to interpret this releasing of prisoners to be about purgatory.

2. But if she did, then Christ would have already led out the prisoners who were there by His blood. Indeed, it is inimical to His

merit when the Roman Church places in purgatory the souls whom Christ has already released.

(a) Bell. l. 4. de Christo cap. 1. Riber. in Zach. 9. num. 52.

[107] (2)"Judas Maccabeus [a] sent 2,000 drachms of silver to Jerusalem as an offering for the sins of the dead."

Answer:

1. No [b] article of faith should properly be proven from the Books of Maccabees.

2. In the Greek text, the work of Judas is merely recounted, not commended.

3. But whether it is commended or not, there is, nonetheless, no such offering instituted by God; it remains a [c] human notion that is to be rejected.

4. Moreover, one finds not a single example in Holy Scripture of any such offering for the dead.

5. Indeed, from this example it does not follow that purgatory exists, nor that the dead themselves for whom Judas gave an offering were being tortured in fire.

(a) 2 Macc. 12:43 seq. (b) dist. 16. cap. 1. canones. gl. atque inter apocrypha. (c) Deu. 4:2; Deu. 12:32; Isa. 29:13.

[108] (3)"In Matthew 5, Christ says: You will not get out of prison until you have paid the last penny."

Answer:

1. No man can pay for his sins by himself, or else [a] he would have no need of a Savior.

2. The prison in this passage (even [b] according to the Roman Church's interpretation) is hell, where no payment can be made and from whence there is no release.

(a) Psa. 69:5; Gal. 2:21. (b) Dionys. Carthus. comm. in h. l. Maldonat.

in h. locum. Jansen. harm. Evangel. cap. 40.

[109] (4) "In Matthew 12:32, the sin against the Holy Spirit will not be forgiven, either in this world or in that one. Since there is a forgiveness of sins in that world, it must take place in purgatory."

Answer:

1. The Roman Church [a] understands this same passage in the following way: Whoever sins against the Holy Spirit [b] has no forgiveness.

2. Thus [c] there is certainly no forgiveness in that world.

3. But even if it were true, why are those who are waiting for forgiveness forced to sit in fire and be purged?

(a) Dionys. Carth. in h. locum. (b) Mark 3:29. (c) 2 Cor. 6:2; Mat. 25:10, 12.

[110] (5) "The quality [a] of every work will be tried by the flames of purgatory in the judgment of God."

Answer:

1. Paul is [b] talking about the flames of trial and tribulation, that is, [c] of the Last Judgment.

2. Also, he is referring only to a person's doctrine as that which must be tried in this way.

3. But the notion that one's doctrine is tried by the flames of purgatory is written nowhere in the Scriptures. Neither does the Roman Church teach such a thing.

(a) 1 Cor. 3:13. (b) Psa. 66:10; Sirach 2:5; Pro. 17:3. (c) Isa. 66:16.

[111] (6) [a] "Those who are under the earth must bend the knee to Christ and [b] give glory to God. That must be a reference to the souls in purgatory."

Answer:

1. The Roman Church [c] is still not certain where purgatory is.

2. Since, according to the Holy Scriptures, the damned in hell will [d] bend the knee to Christ with [e] unspeakable anguish of heart and thus confess God, that is, give Him the glory, there is no need to invent purgatory for this purpose.

(a) Phi. 2:10. (b) Rev. 5:13. (c) Bellarm. lib. 2. de Purgator. cap. 6. (d) Wisdom 5:1 seq. (e) Rom. 14:11.

[112] (7) "St. John saw the souls of the martyrs [a] under the altar, crying out for vengeance on those who had killed them."

Answer:

1. The [b] story of Abel explains this text, without any purgatory.

2. John saw the martyrs under the altar who, according to the Roman Church's [c] own opinion, were not sent to purgatory.

3. Purgatory is thus certainly not under the altar.

4. Nor do the souls complain about any torture.

5. As a token of their innocence, they are given [d] white robes.

6. And the saints [e] are in the presence of God in blessedness. How, then, can they be in purgatory?

(a) Rev. 6:9. (b) Gen. 4:10. (c) Bellar. lib. 2. de Purg. cap. 1. §. haec sentential. (d) v. 11. (e) Rev. 7:13 seq.

The Sixth Chief Point.

Fasting and the Distinction of Foods.

[113] The question is properly this: Should a person fast, [a] as a special form of worship, [b] at certain times, [c] with a distinction of foods?

(a) Bellar. lib. 2. de jejun. cap. 11. §. tertio. (b) cap. 14. (c) cap. 5.

[114] To this we say, no! For even if Christians (1) engage in fasting [a] according to their opportunity and desire, (2) especially [b] with a godly life (3) and [c] constant soberness (4) and [d] diligent watchfulness, lest anyone be offended by food, they still should not allow a false worship to be imposed on them with such fasting.

(a) Acts 10:30; Acts 13:2; Acts 14:23; 1 Cor. 7:5. (b) Isa. 58:6 sq. de consecrat. dist. 7. cap. 25. jejunium. (c) Luke 21:36; Rom. 13:13. de consecr. dist. 5. cap. 18. non dicam. cap. 19. Sunt tibi. (d) Acts 15:20; 1 Cor. 8:13; Rom. 14:21.

[115] (1) Christ never commanded such a fast, but [a] leaves it as a matter of Christian freedom. They should, therefore, [b] remain in this freedom, not allowing [c] human commands to be turned into the worship of God.

(a) Mat. 9:15; Col. 2:16. (b) Gal. 5:1; 1 Cor. 10:29. (c) Mat. 15:9; Isa. 1:12.

[116] (2) And since no one in the early Church knew anything about the papistic fasting, therefore, it is [a] a novelty which secretly crept in from [b] the Jews, [c] the heathen, and [d] the Manichaean and Encratite heretics.

(a) Platina in Telesphoro. (b) Isa. 58:5; Zec. 7:5. Polyd. Vergil. lib. 6. de Invent. cap. 6. (c) Baron. anno 42. §. 29. (d) Baron. anno 173. §. 28. seq. anno 187. §. 1. anno 57. §. 188.

[117] (3) Such a fast is nothing but a doctrine of demons. [a] "In the last times some will depart from the faith and cling to deceiving spirits and doctrines of demons, through those who are liars in hypocrisy and who command to abstain from foods, etc." There is an express prohibition against this: [b] "Let no one make you feel guilty over food and drink."

(a) 1 Tim. 4:1. (b) Col. 2:16.

[118] (4) Christians do not have to concern themselves about food (except for the abuse thereof). It is all the same to God whether a person eats or does not eat, for [a] "the kingdom of God is not a matter of eating and drinking." [b] "Food does not commend us to God. If we eat, we will not be better off for it. If we do not eat, we will not be any worse off for it."

(a) Rom. 14:17. (b) 1 Cor. 8:8.

[119] (5) All creatures [a] that God has given for food [b] may be "enjoyed with thanksgiving." What God [c] "has now cleansed," St. Peter is not to consider unclean. But this truth remains: [d] "To the pure, everything is pure," and [e] "what goes into the mouth does not make a man unclean."

(a) Gen. 1:29,30. (b) 1 Tim. 4:4. (c) Acts 10:15. (d) Titus 1:15. (e) Mat. 15:11.

[120] (6) Fasting is also a hypocritical and superstitious form of worship. It consists in [a] self-chosen worship, [b] a sad countenance, and [c] the martyrdom of the body.[4] [d] All meat is forbidden, and yet [e] fish—which is also meat—is allowed. Meat is forbidden [f] because it gives occasion for evil desires, and yet wine is allowed, [g] which kindles evil desires much more readily.

(a) Col. 2:22, 23. (b) Mat. 6:16. (c) Isa. 58:5. (d) Bellarm. lib. 2. de jejun. cap. 4. §. quare ergo. (e) Num. 11:21,22; 1 Cor. 15:39. (f) Bellarm. l. d. §. respondeo, carnium. (g) dist. 35. c. 6. vinolentum.

4 See Luther's German translation of Isa. 58:5. Is this the sort of fast I should choose, that a man should spend the day doing evil to his body?

The exceptions to the above consist in the following: A person should abstain from food:

[121] (1) When God has forbidden food, as He did [a] in Paradise and [b] in the Levitical Law. Therefore, [c] the Maccabees did right, for they preferred to die rather than to enjoy foods that were forbidden by God. The Israelites [d] committed sin in this regard, for they defied God to give them food that He was not inclined to give them.

(a) Gen. 2:17. (b) Lev. 11:4 ff. (c) 2 Macc. 6:18 ff; 7:1 ff. (d) Num. 11:4, 5; Psa. 78:18; 1 Cor. 10:6.

[122] (2) When a person would [a] honor the heathen idols by eating their sacrifices. Therefore, [b] Tobit, [c] Judith, and [d] Daniel did well, for they abstained from such food.

(a) 1 Cor. 10:21. (b) Tob. 1:12. (c) Judith 12:2. (d) Dan. 1:8.

[123] (3) When [a] a fellow Christian might stumble because of food. It was for this reason that [b] the apostles forbade certain foods for a time.

(a) 1 Cor. 8:9 ff. (b) Acts 15:28, 29.

[124] (4) When food is forbidden for earthly reasons, as, for example, when it is harmful to one's health, etc. Thus, [a] the Rechabites drank no wine, but only on account of their father's prohibition.

(a) Jer. 35:6.

[125] But since God did not forbid any foods in connection with the papistic practice of fasting, and there is no danger of idol worship or of giving offense, and there is no earthly reason to forbid foods, and since the prohibition is to be rejected on the aforementioned grounds, therefore fasting cannot remain at all, much less as a form of worship.

[126] But if you say, "I abstain from the forbidden foods only in obedience to the Christian Church," then here is your answer: Since the papistic fast is a doctrine of demons which has been borrowed

from the heathen, heretics, etc.; since it suspends the ordinance of God and is full of hypocrisy, etc.; therefore, the Christian Church can never command it. And even if she could, no Christian could commit such great wickedness against God by obeying such a command.

The Seventh Chief Point.

The Call of the Church's Ministers.

[127] Just as a house father does not put up with any servants or housekeepers whom he has not hired and selected, so, too, God [a] will not put up with any such workers and housekeepers in His Church whom He has not called to it. [b]"How are they to preach, if they are not sent?" [c]"No one takes this honor for himself, unless he is also called by God, just as Aaron was."

(a) Mat. 4:19; Mat. 9:9; 1 Cor. 3:9; 1 Cor. 4:1; 1 Pet. 5:2. (b) Rom. 10:15. (c) Heb. 5:4.

[128] But the way of the wolf is [a] to come uninvited. [b] They "run when the Lord does not send them," and they [c] "do not enter the sheepfold through the door."

(a) Mat. 7:15. (b) Jer. 23:25. (c) John 10:1.

[129] But when a servant and teacher of the Church is called, he must not wait for such a call as God extended to the prophets and apostles, without intermediaries. He works through means, namely, through the unanimous selection of the entire congregation, that is, of all the estates that belong to it. The teaching estate, as St. Paul [a] appointed Timothy and [b] Titus to the Church office and [c] commanded them to ordain others.

(a) 2 Tim. 1:6. (b) Titus 1:5. (c) 2 Tim. 2:2; Titus 1:5.

[130] The ruling estate, as [a] Solomon, [b] Jehoshaphat, [c] Hezekiah appointed Church offices. [d] The Christian emperors also did this for a long time, [e] until they were dissuaded from such righteousness by the popes.

(a) 1 Kings 2:27,35. (b) 2 Chr. 27:7. (c) 2 Chr. 29:5. (d) dist. 63. cap.

22. Hadrianus. cap. 23. in Synodo, etc. dist. 63. c. 16. Reatina. (e) caus. 16. quaest. 7. cap. 12. Si quis deinceps.

[131] The domestic estate, as [a] the whole congregation helped to choose Matthias for the apostolic office, and [b] the whole congregation sent Paul and other men to Antioch on Church business.

(a) Acts 1:32. (b) Acts 15:22,25.

[132] But where not all the estates are found in the congregation (as, for example, there was no Christian government at the time of the apostolic Church), then those that remain are enough, so that, if there were a group of prisoners in Turkey, where there is neither Christian government nor preaching office, and they chose one from their midst to be the teacher (whether he were a merchant, soldier, etc.) who could provide the necessary care for the others with teaching and the Sacraments, he would be a true minister of the Church, chosen by God.

[133] Accordingly, when the Roman Church still requires in this matter:

(1) That the ministers of the Church (who appoint others to this office) must come in an orderly line of succession from the apostles, she is demanding something that God neither established nor ordained, nor Has he made it in any way necessary. She is also demanding a condition which she herself does not meet, since the Roman Church cannot demonstrate a definite, direct succession for herself at any level of the teaching office. From that it follows that, at this time, no ministers of the Church are found or appointed anywhere in the world.

[134] (2) That the ministers of the Church must be consecrated and ordained. [a]"The apostles laid their hands on them and [b] prayed over them." However, they did this not to turn it into a necessity, but to show [c] that Christians should begin all their tasks, and thus also this holy work, with prayer.

[135] But what the Roman Church prescribes for this consecration—shaving and anointing, etc.—does not pertain to the proper appointment of the ecclesiastical office. Not in the least.

(a) 1 Tim. 4:15. (b) Acts 1:25. (c) Eph. 5:20; Col. 3:17.

The Eighth Chief Point.

Miracles.

Is it necessary for faith, doctrine and call to be confirmed with miracles and to have such evidence as a witness to their legitimacy?

[136] It is not necessary, in these last days, to confirm faith and doctrine through miracles:

[137] (1) Because no such miracles are to be expected from God in the last days. God promised [a] the miracles of Moses ahead of time, and likewise those that would be done [b] by Christ and [c] by the apostles. But there is no such promise about the last days. Therefore, no one can or should be certain of them.

(a) Exo. 3:20; Exo. 4:3 ff. (b) Isa. 35:5, 6. (c) Mark 16:17, 18.

[138] (2) Because in the last days, only false faith will be recognized with miracles, as they have become the signs of false prophets and of the Antichrist. [a] There will arise false Christs and false prophets, who will do great signs and wonders, so that even the elect (if it were possible) will be led astray into error. [b] The coming of the Antichrist takes place according to the working of Satan, with all kinds of lying powers, signs and wonders.

(a) Mat. 24:24. (b) 2 The. 2:9.

[139] (3) Because the divine gift to perform miracles was taken away and finally came to an end after the time of the apostles. Experience teaches—and the Roman Church admits it—that [a] neither the pope [b] nor anyone else (even if [c] there once were a man in India...) is endowed with miraculous gifts, since, if it had been possible, she would have opposed the Lutheran doctrine long ago with miracles, even as, in former times, she (according to [d] her own

fictional accounts) disproved the error of the heretics with miracles.

(a) Lessius disp. de Antichr. dem. 10. p. 58. (b) Greg. de Val. Anal. lib. 6. c. 7. (c) Bell. lib. 4. de not. Eccles. cap. 14. §. denique hoc nostro. (d) Bzovius ann. 1199. §. 43. ann. 1204. §. 23. seq. etc.

[140] (4) Because miracles are a means of demonic deception. For the devil can also do wonders [a] through sorcerers (known examples include [b] Magdalena de la Cruz of Cordoba and [c] others), and also through [d] the heathen and [e] heretics.

(a) Mart. Delrio lib. 1. Mag. disq. cap. 2. p. 3. a Blas. Viega comm. in Apoc. 13. sect. 9. num. 2. Tanner. diopt. l. a. quaest. 4. cap. 28. pag. 619. (b) Zwing. Theatr. p. 1334. b. (c) Bzov. ann. 1199. §. 35. 3. decretal. tit. 45. de reliq. cap. 1. Audivimus. (d) Natal. Com. lib. 6. Mythol. c. 12. pag. 612. (e) Tann. Anat. part. 2. dem. 9. §. 21. Idem, diopt. lib. 2. quaest. 4. cap. 28. pag. 619. Baron. anno 237. §. 8.

[141] (5) Because it can only be known from the Holy Scriptures whether miracles are true or false, for [a] God Himself gave these as signs. [b] Christ proved His wonders from the Scriptures. And [c] Satan masquerades as an angel of light, knowing that human minds cannot always judge sufficiently when it comes to the vanities of street magicians and frivolous games (much less when it comes to Satan's crafty tricks). Moreover, the Roman Church cannot point to any other infallible means by which to distinguish between true and false miracles, as she must confess the truth and, for the sake of this point, [d] direct us to the Holy Scriptures. It follows, then, that what is true of every doctrine is true also of miracles: They can prove nothing to us by themselves; every doctrine must finally stand upon the Holy Scripture alone.

(a) Deu. 13. (b) Mat. 11:4, 5. (c) 1 Cor. 11:13, 14. (d) Casp. Sciop. thaumatolog. cap. 6. pag. 34. 35. Tanner. diopt. lib. 2. quaest. 4. cap. 28. pag. 619.

[142] (6) Indeed, the Roman Church must admit that [a] her miracles do not prove her doctrine to be infallibly certain. She must confess that [b] the people have been fooled by such wonders. So testifies

[c] the beautiful Mary of Regensburg, as well as the Mary of Lübeck on the high altar, who, when the altarpiece is pulled open, turns toward the worshipers, and then turns away from them.

(a) Bellarm. lib. 4. de not. Eccles. cap. 14. §. est autem. Gregor. de Valent. Analys. lib. 1. cap. 7. (b) Grets. lib. 2. de peregrinate. cap. 5. pag. 214. 215. Tanner. diopt. lib. 2. quaest. 4. cap. 28. p. 622. (c) Zwing. Theatr. p. 3140. seq.

[143] It is not necessary to confirm the call to the preaching office with miracles where even one teacher has come to the office through proper means and his doctrine agrees with the divine Word:

[144] (1) Because to demand signs (in order to prove a teacher's call) is a work of [a] the Jews, [b] Pharisees, and [c] unbelievers.

(a) 1 Cor. 1:22. (b) Mat. 12:38. (c) 1 Cor. 14:22.

[145] (2) Because Christians have no ordinance and commandment to test the call in this way.

[146] (3) Because practically none of the prophets who left behind their Scriptures for us proved their call with miracles. [a] John the Baptist also did no miracles, and it is well-known that [b] many people believed in the Lord Jesus and [c] were converted through the apostles without any miraculous work.

(a) John 10:41. (b) John 4:18, 19, 42. (c) Acts 1:37; Acts 16:14; Acts 17:11.

[147] (4) Because even if false teachers confirm their call through miracles, [a] no faith should be placed in them.

(a) Deu. 13:1 ff.; Mat. 24:23 ff.

[148] (5) Because a faith comes, not from miracles, but from the Word.

(a) Rom. 10:17.

The Ninth Chief Point.

Confession.

Should a person make confession, that is, should he recount to a properly consecrated priest the sins of which he knows himself to be guilty, having diligently searched his own conscience?

[149] It is indisputable that every sinner who wants to come to grace [a] must confess his sins to God, as [b] the truly penitent have done. If anyone [c] wants to deny his sinfulness or maintain that he has committed no sin, that person has no forgiveness. [d] "If anyone denies his sins, it will not go well for him. But if he confesses and forsakes them, he will obtain mercy." [e] "If we say that we have no sin, we deceive ourselves and the truth is not in us."

(a) Psa. 32:3 ff; Psa. 51:12 ff; Mat. 6:12. (b) Psa. 38:5; Dan. 9:5; Jer. 14:20; Luke 18:13. (c) Gen. 4:9; Luke 18:11. (d) Pro. 28:13. (e) 1 John 1:8.

[150] Likewise, it is undeniable that the confession that is made to the minister of the Church before receiving the Holy Supper has its value:

1. So that those who want to go to the Holy Sacrament may be sufficiently instructed, if they need it.

2. So that it may be determined how they are all examining themselves and whether they may be admitted to the Holy Supper as worthy guests.

3. So that the preacher may remind his hearers individually of their salvation, where necessary.

4. So that anyone who has a special concern weighing on his heart may reveal it to the minister of the divine Word and consider his counsel.

5. So that God's promise about the most gracious remission of sins might be applied to each one individually.

[151] But when confession is considered [a] necessary for salvation, and especially the kind of confession [b] in which all sins must be recounted and that must be made [c] only to a consecrated priest, then it is unchristian:

(a) Concil. Trident. sess. 14. c. 5 & can. 6. caus. 33. quaest. 3. dist. 1. c. 38. non potest. Bellarm. l. 3. de poenit. cap. 2. (b) Bejerl. Conc. sel. 34. p. 641. (c) Caus. 26. quaest. 6. c. 8. is qui poenitentiam. caus. 33. quaest. 3. dist. 6. c. 1. qui vult.

[152] (1) Because God never commanded that confession be made to a minister of the Church. For although [a] God commanded that the truth be confessed in secular courts; and that [b] each one should confess his sins to one another, as [c] Christ commanded; and [d] Judah, [e] Balaam, [f] Achan, [g] Jonah, etc., all confessed their sins without any such formal confession; nevertheless, there is no divine ordinance concerning ecclesiastical confession, and it is unchristian to make it a necessity without God's instruction.

(a) Sirach 4:14. (b) James 5:16. (c) Mat. 5:24. (d) Gen. 38:26. (e) Num. 22:34. (f) Jos. 7:20. (g) Jonah 1:12.

[153] (2) Because there is no compelling reason why a person must confess to the minister of the Church. For although [a] the power to forgive sins is granted to the apostles; although [b] Christ also sent the lepers to the priests; and [c] commanded that Lazarus, when he was raised from the dead, should be loosed; although [d] the believing Ephesians also confessed what they had done; there does not follow from the apostolic authority any individual private confession. And what was commanded of the priests concerning the lepers does not establish any law for the Christians. The loosing of Lazarus from his grave clothes has not the least thing to do with auricular confession. The fact that the Ephesians confessed their sins does not establish any necessity for other Christians, nor can such a confession

by any means be compelled. That is a Pharisaical burden, a need without cause.

(a) Mat. 18:18; John 20:23. (b) Mat. 8:4; Luke 17:14. (c) John 11:44. (d) Acts 19:18.

[154] (3) Because many people have obtained the forgiveness of sins without individual or private confession: [a] the paralytic, [b] the penitent sinful woman, [and] [c] the evildoer who was crucified with Christ. Nor is there any report that [d] St. Peter, [e] Saul, or [f] the Ethiopian eunuch ever made confession.

(a) Mat. 9:2. (b) Luke 7:47. (c) Luke 23:43. (d) Mat. 26:75. (e) Acts 9:17 ff. (f) Acts 8:37.

[155] (4) And thus we see that, in practice, [a] neither Christ nor [b] the apostles required private confession of the penitent, and certainly not as something necessary. Nor did they direct even a single man to it.

(a) Luke 19:9, 10. (b) Acts 2:38; Acts 16:31.

[156] The private recounting of sins [a] is treated as necessary in the Roman Church. But it is (1) impossible. [b] "Who can mark how often he errs? Pardon my hidden faults." [c] God "sets our unknown sins in the light of His countenance."

(a) Concil. Trident. sess. 14. can. 7. 8. (b) Psa. 19:12. (c) Psa. 90:8.

[157] (2) And since no one can possibly recount all his sins, he would have to constantly waver in doubt, wondering whether he is still under God's wrath due to unconfessed sins. And thus [a] his heart could never again trust firmly in the grace of God.

(a) Heb. 13:9; James 1:6.

[158] (3) It is based neither on commandment, nor promise, nor threat, nor examples in Holy Scripture.

[159] (4) It was not common in the ancient Church; [a] it was sufficient to recognize oneself as a sinner.

(a) 2 Sam. 12:13; Mat. 3:6.

The Tenth Chief Point.

Good Works and Life.

Are good works—in addition to, and apart from, the merit of Christ—not only useful for man's salvation, but also necessary?

[160] There is absolutely no doubt among Christians that they should [a] deny ungodliness and worldly lusts, that they are to [b] die to sin and live to God in righteousness.

(a) Titus 2:12. (b) Rom. 6:11, 13.

[161] It is also certain that good works are necessary, so that a person should (1) [a] render obedience to God, who commanded them; (2) [b] glorify God before the world by means of them; (3) and abandon the sinful behavior that [c] stirs up God's wrath and [d] brings eternal condemnation.

(a) Col. 1:20; Titus 3:8; 1 Pet. 2:24. (b) Mat. 5:16; 1 Pet. 2:12. (c) Rom. 1:18. (d) Rom. 6:11, 13; Rom. 8:6–13. Gal. 5:21; 2 Pet. 2:20, 22.

[162] Moreover, good works have [a] their reward, and [b] even a drink of water shall not remain unrewarded. Therefore, God [c] calls His gracious works a reward, but one which He distributes [d] freely, as [e] an inheritance, [f] not according to merit and righteousness, but only [g] according to His fatherly will.

(a) 2 Cor. 5:10. (b) Mat. 10:42. (c) Gen. 15:1. (d) Rom. 11:35. (e) Mat. 25:34. (f) Mat. 20:15; Mat. 25:21, 33. (g) Mat. 7:9, 11.

[163] Although evil deeds are, indeed, harmful to salvation, good works, nevertheless, are neither useful nor necessary for obtaining it. For:

[164] (1) All that we have received from God [a] comes from His grace. No one can demand his bread from God, but must [b] ask Him

for it, receiving it [c] from His tender kindness. Indeed, we deserve absolutely [d] none of His gracious works. Salvation itself is [e] a gift and [f] an inheritance that is given out of pure grace. [g] "By grace you have been saved, through faith—and that not of yourselves; it is the gift of God—not by works, lest anyone should boast." [h] "But if it is by grace, then it is not by works, or else grace would not be grace."

(a) 1 Cor. 4:7. (b) Mat. 6:11. (c) Psa. 145:15, 16. (d) Gen. 32:10. (e) Rom. 6:23. (f) Mat. 25:34. (g) Eph. 2:8. (h) Rom. 11:6.

[165] (2) Christ redeemed us [a] so that, through Him, we might have the salvation that He, [b] by grace, [c] will give us. How, then, can the merits of works be either useful or necessary to that end?

(a) Acts 4:12. (b) John 1:16, 17. (c) John 10:18.

[166] (3) Besides the grace of God and the merit of Christ, salvation is ascribed only to faith. [a] We maintain that man is justified only by faith, without the works of the Law. [b] All who believe in the Son shall have eternal life. [c] Whoever believes in Him is not judged. [d] Whoever believes and is baptized will be saved. [e] The end of faith is the salvation of your souls. Since, then, on this point, [f] faith and good works exclude each other, it follows that works do not serve at all for salvation.

(a) Rom. 3:28. (b) John 3:16. (c) John 3:18, 36. (d) Mark 16:16. (e) 1 Pet. 3:9. (f) Rom. 11:6.

[167] (4) If good works are to serve for salvation, then they must be completely perfect, so that no sinful uncleanness clings to them. But now [a] the righteousnesses of the saints (that is, their highest and best works) are like a filthy garment. And [b] in whatever man undertakes, something unclean always clings to it. No sin may exist alongside the good works, for [c] he who sins in one thing [d] is cursed. And [e] all men alike are sinners, so that [f] all the saints must ask for the forgiveness of sins. It follows infallibly that no one's good works can be useful for salvation.

(a) Isa. 64:6. (b) Sirach 27:5; Rom. 7:21. (c) James 2:10. (d) Deu. 27:26; Gal. 3:10. (e) Rom. 3:23; 1 John 1:8; Ecc. 7:21. (f) Psa. 32:6; Mat. 6:12.

[168] (5) But even if everyone were perfectly pious (which is, of course, [a] impossible), he would still [b] only be doing his duty. Indeed, he would [c] not even deserve thanks, much less eternal salvation.

(a) Rom. 8:3; Acts 13:38. (b) Luke 17:10. (c) Luke 17:9.

[169] (6) The Holy Scriptures testify strongly that righteousness and salvation [a] do not come by works of the Law, nor [b] by a single work of man; these are entirely excluded from the matter of our salvation. [c] "He saved us, not for the sake of works of righteousness which we had done, but according to His mercy." [d] "We maintain that man is justified without the works of the Law." [e] Abraham was justified without works, as were [f] Saul, [g] the tax collector, [h] the evil-doer who was crucified with Christ, etc. None of that could have happened if good works were necessary for salvation.

(a) Gal. 4:11, 21. (b) Rom. 4:6. (c) Titus 3:5. (d) Rom. 3:28. (e) Gen. 15:6; Rom. 4:2, 3. (f) Acts 9:3 ff. (g) Luke 18:13,14. (h) Luke 23:43.

[170] (7) Indeed, those who seek life and salvation in good works [a] do not obtain righteousness, but [b] have lost Christ. They have [c] fallen from grace and are [d] under God's curse. Again it follows: The works that are done as useful or as necessary for salvation are actually most harmful to it.

(a) Rom. 4:4; Rom. 9:31, 32; Luke 18:11, 14. (b) Gal. 5:4; Gal. 2:21. (c) Gal. 5:4. (d) Gal. 3:10.

The Eleventh Chief Point.

The Antichrist.

Is the Roman pope the Antichrist?

[171] Although [a] all heretics are antichrists, there is [b] one great, eminent world-deceiver whom the Holy Spirit calls Antichrist. His coming was prophesied and indicated with particular marks that should serve as signs, all of which are found in this man who is, without doubt, the great Antichrist.

(a) 1 John 2:18. (b) 2 The. 2; 1 John 2:18, 22.

[172] It has been sufficiently demonstrated by others that these signs point to the Roman pope. And since this is not the place to give a detailed explanation of the same, it will be enough to show that the sixteen proofs which the unnamed author introduces are not helpful to the pope, but that he, in spite of such "proofs," still remains the Antichrist.

[173] (1) "The Antichrist is supposed to be a single person (John 5, 2 The. 2, 1 John 2). There have been 240 popes."

Answer:

1. No one can prove that the Antichrist will be only one person. For [a] when the Lord Christ says, "If another comes in his own name, you will receive him," He is speaking of all those who will introduce themselves as Christ, [b] of whom there would be many. Indeed, [c] the Holy Scriptures name some of them.

2. The Antichrist is [d] described as one (on account of the office and order), and yet [e] also as many (according to the persons).

3. Therefore, although there is only one pope, according to the practice of the papal empire, just as in the Roman empire there

is only one emperor, and [f] in the Jewish synagogue there is only one high priest, there still remains one Antichrist who reveals himself little by little in many persons. And thus, when the Roman Church treats of the papal office, [g] she recognizes only one pope, no matter how many of them have come before.

(a) John 5:43. (b) Mat. 24:24. (c) Acts 5:36,37. (d) 2 The. 2:3, 4. (e) Mat. 24:24. (f) Lev. 21:10. (g) dist. 99. c. 5. Ecce, in. Mussus Conc. de nativ. p. 31. Bellarm. lib. 4. de Rom. Pont. cap. 1. seq.

[174] (2) "The Antichrist will not come until the great falling away from the Roman empire[5] takes place (Dan. 7, 2 The. 2). This has not yet happened."

Answer: [a] The prophecy of falling away [b] properly concerns the Christian faith. But if someone wanted to understand it as falling away from the Roman empire (which St. Paul had in view [c] when he said, "You know that which still holds it back"), he should know that it is not the complete demise of the Roman empire that is foretold (since it is to [d] endure until the Last Day), but a reduction of its great authority, on account of which the Antichrist at first could not come to power. The falling away took place, in part, when a number of kings fell away from the Roman empire, diminishing its strength; in part, when the one empire was divided into two separate empires—the eastern and the western. [e] The western empire came to an end in the year A.D. 475 with Emperor Augustulus, and then rose again with Charlemagne (320 years later). At this falling away, the Antichrist, under the confusion caused by the Goths and Exarchs, was able to rise to power, and the popes have taken this opportunity to increase their authority greatly.

(a) 2 The. 2:3. (b) 2 The. 2:10 ff.; 1 Tim. 4:1. (c) 2 The. 2:6. (d) Dan. 2:34; Dan. 7:8,9. (e) Bellar. Chronol. part. 2. ad ann. 476. Tanner. diopt. lib. 3. quaest. 3. cap. 14. p. 955.

[175] (3) "The Antichrist will not come [a] before the Gospel has

5 *Reich*

been thoroughly preached in the whole world (Mat. 24). But now, to this very day, there are new islands and tribes being discovered where the Gospel is being introduced for the first time."

Answer: Since [b] the apostles were commanded to preach the Gospel in the whole world, [c] which they did willingly and well, [d] as the Roman Church cannot deny—especially if she wants to be called "Catholic," [e] stretching out into the whole world (which [f] cannot happen without the preaching of the Gospel)—and since one finds signs of Christianity even now in territories that were previously unknown, such as in the [g] East Indies (where St. Thomas and Bartholomew and Matthew were supposed to have preached), as well as in the [h] West Indies and China, etc., there is no need for any new preaching to take place throughout the world (in order to fulfill Christ's prophecy). This is enough, and was all carried out gloriously before the papal empire ever began.

(a) Mat. 24:14. (b) Mat. 28:19; Mark 16:15. (c) Rom. 10:18; Col. 1:6,23. (d) Jansen. harmon. Evang. cap. 122. p. 94. Bisciola, Epit. annal. Baron. pag. 28. d. (e) Tanner. diopt. l. 2. quaest. 4. cap. 23. pag. 520. Bellar. lib. 4. de Notis Eccles. cap. 7. (f) Rom. 10:14,17. (g) Grets. defens. 2. lib. 3. cap. 4. pag. 855. c. d. (h) Nicol. Trigautius de exped. ad Sinas, l. 2. c. 11. p. 121. seq.

[176] (4) "Before the Antichrist comes, the two great saints, Enoch and Elijah, must appear again in the world and preach (Rev. 11). That did not occur prior to any pope."

Answer:

1. The Roman Church herself has no certain teaching about this. Some think [a] that Moses will appear with Elijah; others suggest [b] Jeremiah instead; most add a third, namely, [c] John the Theologian; some maintain that [d] these witnesses have nothing to do with the Antichrist. They should first come to some agreement on this matter.

2. But that [e] the Antichrist will be opposed by two wit-

nesses, namely, the confessors of the truth, of whom the Antichrist will kill many—and [f] the pope has fulfilled this prophecy diligently enough—is beyond controversy.

3. It is impossible to prove that these witnesses must be Enoch and Elijah.

4. That which was prophesied [g] concerning Elijah's return [h] was fulfilled in John the Baptist. Enoch's coming is never mentioned.

5. In addition, since Enoch and Elijah [i] now have immortal bodies, therefore they cannot be killed. Thus, they cannot be the two witnesses [j] whom the Antichrist will kill.

(a) Less. de Antichr. dem. 15. p. 141. Viega in Apoc. 11. sect. 7. (b) Viega ib. Tyraeus disp. de Antichr. cap. 19. §. 306. (c) Viega in Apoc. 10. sect. 8. num. 1. (d) Alcasar proleg. in Apoc. notat. 20. §. 1. Rev. 11:3. (e) Rev. 11:7; Rev. 17:6. (f) Catalog. Test. Verit. (g) Mal. 4:5. (h) Mat. 17:11, 13. (i) Mat. 22:30; 1 Cor. 15:52 ff. (j) Rev. 11:7.

[177] (5) "The Antichrist is supposed to come from ignoble descent and usurp the Jewish kingdom through deceit. He is also supposed to wage war against three kings—of Egypt, of Libya, and of Ethiopia—whom he will overpower. Likewise, he will bring seven others under his power, and finally persecute Christians everywhere on earth by strength of battle (Dan. 7 & 11; Rev. 20). This does not agree at all with the pope."

Answer:

1. There is no prophecy about the Antichrist saying that he will usurp the Jewish kingdom.

2. The pope did, indeed, come from a lowly estate (since [a] he was only the Bishop of Rome and [b] was equal to the others) to rise, through deceit, high above all the world's nobility, like the fraudulent fable [c] that Emperor Constantine had given him the entire Roman Empire in the West for his own, etc.

3. The war [d] against Egypt, Libya, and Ethiopia, etc., is properly a prophecy concerning King Antiochus. But he is, indeed, a type of the Antichrist, and it is also thereby prophesied about him that he will force the kingdoms to submit to him with power and with war. [e] To the extent that is properly interpreted, it is known all over the world how the pope, [f] with immeasurable bloodshed, has not only made Sicily his own, but has also made the Roman emperors and other kings subject to him with bloody wars.

4. The pope ([g] as the Antichrist) has thereby become a world monarch, so that [h] all kings and potentates, [i] all peoples, [j] all churches, [k] all Christians, and, in short, [l] the entire face of the earth must be subject to him.

(a) Nic. Conc. can. 6. Tom. 1. Conc. pag. 253. (b) dist. 93. cap. 24. legimus. (c) dist. 96. cap. 14. Constantinus. (d) Dan. 11:43. (e) Rev. 13:7; Rev. 17:15. (f) vide Annal. Baronii & Bzovii. (g) Rev. 17:15. (h) Extrav. comm. lib. 1. tit. 8. de major. & obed. cap. 1. Unam sanctam. (i) caus. 1. quaest. 7. cap. 37. beati. (j) caus. 17. quaest. 6. cap. 6. si fortassis. (k) dist. 81. cap. 15. si qui sunt. (l) 5. decret. tit. 12. de homic. volunt. cap. 6. sicut dignum.

[178] (6) "The Antichrist will directly oppose Christ and will pretend to be Christ (1 John 2). What pope has ever done that?"

Answer:

1. It is not written anywhere that the Antichrist will pretend to be Christ.

2. But the Antichrist [a] will directly oppose Christ. The pope does this in that [b] he tears God's ordinance away from Him and [c] despises it. He openly introduces into the Christian Church [d] heathen abominations and Jewish superstitions which Christ rejected. He has very nearly nullified the merits of Christ by commending the merits of the saints. This was treated [e] above.

3. And although he claims with words [f] to be a servant of Christ, [g] he denies it with deeds, just as [h] all heretics battle against

Christ and yet [i] pretend to be His apostles. Lest anyone should notice this, the Antichrist dresses himself [j] like a lamb, with outward holiness.

(a) 2 The. 2:4. (b) Mat. 26:26, 27. vide supra num. 15. (c) Gen. 2:24. dist. 82. cap. 2. proposuisti. (d) supra num. 29. (e) num. 91. (f) l. 1. decretal. tit. 33. de majorit. & obed. cap. 6. solicitae. (g) Titus 2:16. (h) Luke 2:34. (i) 2 Cor. 11:13. (j) Rev. 13:11.

[179] (7) "The Antichrist is supposed to sit in the temple of God in Jerusalem (2 The. 2, Rev. 11). But the pope sits in Rome."

Answer:

1. The Roman Church is not certain in what kind of temple the Antichrist will sit.

2. The Antichrist [a] will, indeed, sit in the temple of God, but there is not a word anywhere in Holy Scripture about that temple being the one in Jerusalem.

3. Since, in the New Testament, there is no temple except for [b] the spiritual, living temple of God (which is [c] the hearts of believers, that is, [d] the communion of saints), to sit in God's temple means nothing other than [e] to rule in the Christian Church (as is understood [f] from the ancient teachers of the Church). That is most assuredly fulfilled [g] in the pope, without exception.

(a) 1 The. 2:4. (b) 1 Cor. 3:16, 17; 1 Cor. 6:9; 2 Cor. 6:19. (c) Eph. 3:17. (d) Mat. 18:20; John 14:23. (e) 1 Kings 1:30; Mat. 23:2. (f) Viega, comm. 2. in Apoc. 13. sect. 8. num. 1. (g) caus. 14. q. 1. c. 14. relatum est.

[180] But the proper seat of the Antichrist is [a] the spiritual Babylon, [b] which is Rome. [c] The seven hills also [d] stand for Rome. The city that [e] rules over the kings of the earth—[f] that is Rome. The city [g] in which our Lord was crucified [h] is not Jerusalem, [i] but Rome, as [j] the ancient teachers of the Church also held in common. Thus, the pope's current seat is the seat of the Antichrist.

(a) Rev. 17:5. (b) Bell. l. 2. de Rom. Pontif. cap. 2. Gretser. defens. 2. contr. lib. 2. cap. 2. (c) Rev. 17:19. (d) Bellarm. lib. 3. de Rom. Pontif. cap. 5. §. denique. Tyraeus disput. de Antichristo c. 11. §. 137. (e) Rev. 17:18. (f) Polyd. Vergil. lib. 8. de Invent. cap. 7. p. 654. (g) Rev. 11:8. (h) Bellar. lib. 3. de Rom. Pontif. cap. 13. §. quare. Viega in Apoc. 11. sect. 12. num. 1. (i) 4. deret. tit. 17. qui matrim. accus. cap. 13. per venerab. Platina in vita D. Petri. (j) Tyraeus, disput. de Antichr. cap. 11. p. 140. Tanner. Anat. part. 2. dem. 5. §. 281.

[181] (8) "The Antichrist will allow himself to be worshiped as God (2 The. 2). No pope has ascribed to himself such a thing."

Answer: The Antichrist [a] rules in God's Church as God and pretends to be God, not only by allowing himself [b] to be formally called a god or by pretending that he is actually [c] taking the place of God as [d] the Bridegroom of the Christian Church, which applies [e] to Christ alone, but also by leading his government as a god, so that he extends his power [f] over the whole world and refuses [g] to be bound by any laws or [h] to be subject to any man. He who ascribes all this to himself rules in Christ's Church as a god.

(a) 2 The. 2:4. (b) dist. 96. cap. 7. satis evidenter. (c) lib. 1. decret. tit. 7. de transact. Episc. cap. quanto persona. (d) Extrav. Johan. 22. tit. 5. de sed. vac. cap. 1. si fratrum. (e) John 3:29; Eph. 5:25 ff. (f) lib. 1. decret. tit. 6. de elect. cap. 3. ubi periculum. (g) l. 3. decret. tit. 2. de concess. praeb. cap. 4. proposuit. (h) Sext. lib. 1. tit. 6. de elect. cap. 17. fundamenta.

[182] (9) "The Antichrist will exalt and raise himself above God and above all that is or is called God (2 The. 2). No pope does that; he presents himself as a minister of all God's servants."

Answer: St. Paul's [a] prophecy says: "The opponent exalts himself over everything that is called God or the worship of God." The pope has now exalted himself over God the Most High by taking away [b] the cup of the Lord's Supper, which Christ ordained and from which [c] Christ commanded to drink. He [d] forbids marriage, which God wants to be [e] held sacred and [f] to be left unforbidden.

The pope makes Christians feel guilty [g] about eating and drinking where God [h] wants no one to make another feel guilty. He [i] forbids anyone to examine and to judge him when he leads astray countless souls into the depths of hell, although [j] Christ wants all spirits to be tested. And then he [k] casts away penitent sinners when God [l] wants to receive them into grace. Not to mention how the will of God is made secondary to everything else, while the pope's commands against God advance unhindered. Is that not rightly called exalting himself over God? In the same way, he has also [m] exalted himself over all authorities [n] that are called gods.

(a) 2 The. 2:4. (b) Conc. Const. Sess. 13. (c) Mat. 26:27. (d) caus. 32. quaest. 2. cap. 4. connubial. (e) Heb. 13:4. (f) Gen. 2:24. (g) de consec. dist. 5. cap. 31. qui dies. (h) Col. 2:16; 1 Tim. 4:3, 4. (i) dist. 40. c. 6. Si Papa. (j) Mat. 17:15; 1 John 4:1; 1 The. 5:20. (k) Wolf lect. memor. Cent. 6. 172. (l) Mat. 11:28; John 6:37. (m) dist. 96. cap. 11. Si Imperator. cap. 10. nunquam. 1. decretal. tit. 6. cap. 34. venerabilem. (n) Psa. 82:1.

[183] (10) "The Jews are supposed to accept the Antichrist as their Messiah (John 5). They have thus far never accepted any pope."

Answer: There is no word to be found in Holy Scripture concerning this Messiah of the Jews. For [a] when the Lord Christ says, "I have come in My Father's name, and you do not receive Me. If another comes in his own name, you will receive him," there is no reason to understand this concerning the Antichrist. Indeed, it is well-known how this was fulfilled by false christs to whom the Jews clung, to their own destruction, namely, [b] Theudas, Judas of Galilee, [c] Moses of Egypt, [d] Barcochab, etc.

(a) John 5:43. (b) Acts 5:36, 37. (c) Socrat. lib. 7. hist. Eccl. cap. 37. (d) Zwing. Theatr. p. 902.

[184] (11) "The Antichrist will work miraculous signs through sorcery and Satanic arts (Mat. 24; 2 The. 2; Rev. 11). The popes do their miraculous signs in the name of Jesus and condemn sorcery."

Answer:

1. The Antichrist's coming is to take place [a] according to the working of Satan, with all kinds of lying signs and wonders.

2. There is no doubt that the pope does wonders, since the Roman Church wants [b] to be recognized as Christ's Church by means of those very wonders. Indeed, there is no end to the reports of the miracles of [c] the Mary of Loretto, of [d] the Mary of Hall, of Oettingen, etc., how all the miracles take place [e] near many graves and bones, whereby [f] the Antichrist would secure his reign, etc.

3. If the pope's miraculous signs do not come from God, [g] as demonstrated above, then they must stem from the deceit of Satan, etc., as [h] the Magdalene from Creutz, the beautiful Mary of Regensburg, and others testify that such demonic works are done regularly in the Roman Church, especially since [i] the Lord Christ specifically warned us about the miracles of the end time. Nor does it make any difference whether the pope misuses the name of the Lord Jesus for this purpose, for so do all sorcerers as well. Indeed, their sin is that much worse because of it.

(a) 2 The. 2:9. (b) Bellarm. lib. 4. de Notis Eccles. cap. 14. (c) Horat. Tursell. historia Laurentana. (d) Grets. lib. 2. de sacr. peregr. cap. 6. etc. (e) Tanner. diopt. lib. 2. cap. 29. p. 634 seq. (f) Blas. Viega in Apocal. 13. sect. 11. num. 1. (g) num. 137. seq. (h) supra, num. 142. (i) Mat. 24:24.

[185] (12) "The Antichrist will raise himself up and put himself forth (Dan. 11; 2 The. 2). The Roman popes are elected properly and in an orderly way."

Answer: Here a distinction must be made between the person of the pope and his office. On account of the office, they have exalted themselves to both spiritual and secular power. To spiritual power, because [a] God has given him no authority over all churches. For this reason, [b] the Fathers did not presume such authority for themselves, and if anyone attempted to do so, he was rightly recognized, [c] not as a servant of Christ, but [d] as the Antichrist himself. Nor has God given the pope [e] any secular power in the governance of the world. Therefore, since he (contrary to divine order) wants to rule [f] over all the churches of the world and [g] forcefully subject all Christians to himself, [h] and since he does whatever he wishes in the secular government, it is evident that the pope is raising himself up and putting himself forth for his office, without a divine call.

(a) dist. 93. cap. 24. legimus. caus. 24. quaest. 1. c. 18. loquitur. dist. 99. cap. 4. nullus Patriarchar. (b) Greg. de Val. Anal. lib. 7. c. 13. p. 85. b. (c) dist. 40. c. 12. multi sacerdot. (d) dist. 99. c. 5. ecce. Greg. Magn. Epist. 6. ad Maurit. Imp. (e) Luke 22:25,26. caus. 33. quaest. 2. cap.6. inter haec. Tanner. diopt. lib. 3. quaest. 2. cap. 8. p. 861. (f) Extrav. com. lib. 2. tit. 2. c. 2. ex supernae. (g) Extrav. com. lib. 1. tit. 8. c. 1. Unam sanctam. (h) lib. 5. decret. tit. 39. de sentient. excommunicate. cap. 53. gravem. Clement. lib. 2. tit. 11. cap. 2. pastoralis. Extravag. Joh. 22. tit. 5. ne sede vac. cap. 1. si fratrum.

[186] With regard to their person, the popes rarely come to their office through a proper and orderly election. I will demonstrate this at the present time from the single historical writer, Platina. He testifies [a] universally that, at the time of Stephen VI and afterward, the papacy was obtained among the clergy through bribery, selfish ambition, and violence. [b] Felix II, in particular, went from heretic to pope, having also acquired his position of power through improper and disorderly means. [c] Damasus II obtained the papacy through violence and weapons; [d] Silverius, also through violence; [e] Vigilius I, through violence; [f] Sergius I, through bribery; [g] Martin II, through evil tricks; [h] Formosus I, through gifts; [i] Stephen VI, through bribery; [j] Leo V, through violence and insurrection; [k] Sergius III, through gifts and selfish ambition; (around the same time [l] it became commonplace for the popes to rise to power through bribery and raging ambition); [m] Christopher I, through evil deeds; [n] John XI, through violence; [o] Benedict V, through violence and insurrection; [p] Gregory

V, through his relation to Emperor Otto III; [q] John XVIII, through deceitful tricks, selfish ambition, lust for power, bribery, and the aid of the devil. So, too, [r] Sylvester II and [s] Sylvester III rose to the papal throne through gifts; [t] Damasus II, through open violence; [u] Victor II, through friendship with Emperor Henry; [v] Benedict X, through violence and bribery; [w] Honorius II, through raging ambition and other deceitful tricks; [x] Gregory X, through the disunity and strife among the cardinals; [y] Boniface VIII, through deceitful tricks; [z] John XXIV, through bribery. The most recent popes, Leo XI and Paul V, (according to [aa] the testimony of the cardinals of Joyeuse and Cardinal du Perron) were elected more to address the financial needs of the potentates and the cardinals than for the welfare of the Christian Church. [bb] Gregory XV was exalted to the papal throne amid great controversy, through a crooked election, not in view of the Church's wellbeing, but on account of secular dealings. Similarly, the current pope, [cc] Urban VIII, became pope amid the cardinals' despicable quarreling and back-biting. Yes, they have such good reason to boast about their proper and orderly election!

(a) in vita Steph. 6. pag. 145. b. (edit. Col. anni. 16oc.) Silvestri 3. pag. 168. b. Damas. 2. pag. 170. b. (b) p. 51. a. seq. (c) p. 53. b. (d) pag. 75. b. (e) p. 77. (f) pag. 103. b. (g) p. 142. a.b. (h) p. 144. b. (i) pag. 145. b. (j) pag. 148. (k) pap. 149. b. (l) pag. 148. a. (m) pag. 148. (n) pag. 151. a. (o) pag. 156. (p) pag. 161. b. (q) pag. 164. b. (r) pag. 163. b. (s) pag. 169. (t) pag. 170. (u) pag. 182. (v) pag. 173. (w) pag. 196. a. (x) pag. 233. b. (y) pag. 246. a. (z) pag. 283. b. (aa) in Epistolis ad Gall. Regem, idiomate Gallico scriptis. (bb) Johannes Ludovicus Gotofredus, Archontolog. pag. 57. seq. (cc) ibid. pag. 66.

[187] (13) "The Antichrist will persecute the saints (Dan. 7; Mat. 24; Rev. 20). The pope does not do that."

Answer: The true holiness of Christians consists (1) in [a] the holiness won by Christ and distributed through Word and Sacrament; (2) in [b] the indwelling of God and the communion of the Holy Spirit; (3) in [c] the holy Word and doctrine; (4) in [d] God's holy call; (5) in [e] holy divine worship; (6) in [f] holy life and conduct (but [g] not in the manner of hypocrites). Now, then, since the pope (although he can suffer the Jews gladly enough) pursues and persecutes those who recognize and honor the Lord Jesus alone as their propitiation[6] and sanctification (having rejected all the holiness of men), it is clear that the pope persecutes the saints, fulfilling also this sign of the Antichrist.

(a) Isa. 4:3.4; Isa. 62:12; 1 Cor. 1:30; Heb. 10:14; Col. 1:22. (b) 1 Cor. 3:17; Psa. 51:12. (c) John 17:17; 2 The. 2:13. (d) Rom. 1:7. (e) Psa. 110:3; Eze. 37:28; Joel 3:17. (f) 1 The. 4:3,4; 1 Pet. 1:15; Col. 3:12. (g) Isa. 58:5; Mat. 6:1, 5, 16; Col. 2:21 ff.

[188] (14) "The Antichrist will abolish the sacrifice of the holy Mass (Dan. 12). The pope does not do that; quite the opposite."

Answer:

1. Daniel prophesied that King Antiochus would do away with [a] the daily sacrifice ordained by God, which [b] he abundantly fulfilled. That is [c] the common interpretation of the Roman Church.

2. Just as Antiochus is a picture of the Antichrist, so the Levitical daily sacrifice is a picture, not of the Mass, but of [d] the holy sacrifice of Christ on the cross. Accordingly, [e] the Antichrist will abolish this, since, apart from this one sacrifice, [f] there is nothing else in Christendom that is properly called a sacrifice.

3. Clearly the Antichrist cannot actually abolish Christ's sacrifice. He can only rip it out of people's hearts, which the pope does when he directs Christians to place their confidence [g] more in the Virgin Mary, in the intercession of other saints, or in their own merits, rather than in the suffering of Christ. This is common knowledge.

4. Since the Mass is a truly Antichristian work, it cannot be the sacrifice meant in Daniel's prophecy.

---

6 *Sündenbüsser*

5. On the contrary, [h] what is prophesied is that the Antichrist will honor his god Mausim[7] (who was unknown to the Fathers) with gold, silver, precious stones, and pleasant things, and that he will distribute the land to those who help him strengthen this god Mausim. Since, then, the bread of the Mass [i] is worshiped as a god, who was [j] unknown to the holy apostles and to the early Christians, and is also honored with gold, silver, etc., it seems that Daniel prophesied that the Antichrist would not do away with the Mass, but would establish it, as the pope has done.

(a) Exo. 28:3 ff. (b) Maccab. 1:23, etc. (c) Viega Comm. 2. in Apoc. 13. sect. 12. num. 1. (d) Col. 2:16, 17; Heb. 10:1. (e) Dan. 11:31. (f) supra, num. 74. (g) Himmel. de Invoc. Sanct. part. 2. class. 3. c. 1. p. 292. seq. 297. sq. (h) Dan. 11:38,39. (i) Bellarm. lib. 4. de Eucharist. cap. 29. (j) supra, num. 79.

[189] (15) "The Antichrist is only supposed to reign for three and a half years (Dan. 7:12, Rev. 11:13). But the popes have ruled for about 1600 years now."

Answer:

1. Since the Roman Church [a] has never been certain about this reckoning of years, she cannot force this interpretation on anyone so strongly.

2. The prophecies [b] declare that the deception should last for "a time, two times, and half a time," which is [c] 42 months or [d] 1,260 days. This cannot be understood according to the common division of years, days, and months, (1) for in such little time the Antichrist could not influence the world (for whose conversion [e] the apostles worked twenty years). (2) If the Antichrist [f] is supposed to draw the Jews to himself (as the Roman Church imagines) and [g] build himself a temple in Jerusalem (although it took [h] seven years

---

7 See Luther's German translation of Dan. 11:38. *Aber an des Statt wird er seinen Gott Maußim ehren; denn er wird einen Gott, davon seine Väter nichts gewußt haben, ehren mit Gold, Silber, Edelstein und Kleinoden.*

to build the first temple and [i] 46 years to build the second), when would he rule in it? (3) In addition, if this wretchedness was already stirring [j] at the time of St. Paul and will only [k] come to an end on the Last Day, it is impossible to wrap it up into three and a half years.

3. If the days (according to [l] the pattern of the Scriptures) are reckoned as years, then the Antichrist shall reign for 1,260 or (counting one year as 365 years) for 1,277 years.

4. Thus it is either being viewed from the time of complete rule, which began [m] with Boniface III, c. A.D. 607, until the year 1867; or from the time when [n] the dispersion[8] of the holy people came to an end under Emperor Constantine, when the papal reign began to exalt itself with violence, until the time of his revelation, which occurred in the 16th century in the year 1572.

5. One should not be overly concerned that the dates do not match up precisely, for [o] the prophecies have not yet been clarified and explained through fulfillment and the conclusion of time.

(a) Viega in Apoc. 20. Comm. 1. sect. a. §. 12. 13. Alcasar in h. l. com. p. 525. c. d. (b) Dan. 12:7; Rev. 12:14. (c) Rev. 11:2. (d) Rev. 11:2. (e) Bell. l. 3. de Rom. Pont. c. 4. §. deinde, tribus. (f) vide supra num. 138. (g) Bellarm. lib. 3. de Rom. Pont. c. 13. Viega in Apoc. 13. com. 2 sect. 7. §. 1. 2. (h)1 Kings 6:38. (i) John 2:20. (j) 2 The. 2:7. (k) 2 The. 2:8. (l) Lev. 25:3 ff.; Eze. 4:6; Dan. 9:24, 25. (m) Platina in vita Bonif. 3. p. 85. (n) Dan. 12:7. (o) Dan. 12:4,9.

[190] (16) "The Last Judgment is supposed to come immediately after the Antichrist (Dan. 7; Mat. 24; 2 The. 2). We have not yet seen this. Therefore, the pope is not the Antichrist."

Answer: St. Paul [a] expressly prophesied about this: "Whom the Lord will slay with the Spirit of His mouth and destroy by the appearance of His coming." So if the evil [b] was stirring at the time

---

8 See Luther's German translation of Daniel 12:7. ...*und wenn die Zerstreuung des heiligen Volks ein Ende hat, soll solches alles geschehen.* "...and when the dispersion of the holy people comes to an end, all this shall take place."

of the apostle, and was to be revealed in due time, but only [c] entirely destroyed at the Last Day, then one cannot conclude anything about how near or far the Last Day may be from the Antichrist's coming and revelation. It merely follows that the Antichrist will cause the final turmoil and sorrow in the Christian Church. That is being plentifully fulfilled before our very eyes. God have mercy on His imperiled Church and deliver her by His glorious appearing! Amen.

(a) 2 The. 2:8. (b) 2 The. 2:7. (c) Tyraeus disp. de Antichr. c. 9. §. 84. Less. de Antichr. demonstr. 16. p. 175.

Conclusion

The following conclusion is drawn from all of this:
The Church that:

1. Can be shown, with solid evidence, to be unchristian;
2. Twists the holy institution of the Lord's Supper into a blasphemous sacrifice;
3. Promotes superstition through the invocation of saints;
4. Is founded on the unchristian fiction of purgatory;
5. Teaches the doctrine of demons with fasting and the distinction of foods;
6. Questions the call of the Christian Church's ministers without need and without good reason;
7. Does miraculous signs, which are the marks of false doctrine;
8. Turns confession into a stumbling block for consciences;
9. Makes good works necessary for salvation;
10. Recognizes the great Antichrist and deceiver of the world as her supreme head;

... is not the Church of Christ. Therefore, every Christian should most urgently flee and avoid her.

The Roman Church does all these things, as demonstrated above. It follows, then, that the Roman Church is not the Church of Christ. Therefore, all Christians should most urgently flee and avoid her.

Psalm 70:5

My helper and deliverer, my God, do not delay!

A Catholic Answer to the Heretical Question of the Jesuits: Where Was the True Religion and Church before the Time of Luther?

To all the Evangelical Christians suffering under the Papacy

1627

Presented by

Balthasar Meisner

Doctor and Professor of Holy Scripture at Wittenberg

translated by

Paul A. Rydecki

2017

Original title: *Catholische Antwort auf die Ketzerische Frage der Jesuwider, Wo die wahre Religion und Kirche vor Lutheri Zeiten gewesen sey?*

Question: Where was the true Church and the right religion before Luther's time?

It is the practice of the papists, and especially of the Jesuits[1], when they hope to lead simple hearts away from the Evangelical truth, to argue very little from the Holy Scriptures. Instead, they bring up all kinds of crafty questions, which appear on the outside to be innocent enough, but which are posed for no other reason than to lead pious Christians away from the written Word of God and to send them tumbling into wild and useless discussions.

The question presented above is one such question, and they know how to make a great show of it."For," they say,"the Christian Church has the promise that she will always remain, and that she will not be overcome by the gates of hell (Mat. 16:18). But she cannot exist without the true faith. Therefore, it follows that, just as the Church has always remained, so, too, the right religion must have remained on earth. Now, tell us, you Lutherans, where was your religion to be found before Luther's time? Show us a country, show us a single city, show us many or even a few individuals who were devoted to your faith in each and every article! You have no answer, do you? Nothing to say? Our papal religion, on the other hand, has spread out into all the world. The Roman Church alone held the square before Luther. In all of Christendom, in every place, no other faith was preached and heard but the Roman faith. We conclude with certainty, therefore, that our Church must be the apostolic Church, and our faith the right catholic faith. For either the Christian Church, together with the truth, entirely vanished before

---

1 Meisner's term for the Jesuits throughout this book is the derogatory *Jesuwider*, a play on the word *Jesuiter*, meaning "against Jesus."

Luther's time, which goes against the divine promise, or the Lutheran faith and the Lutheran Church have always existed, which goes against experience and history. There is no way to sugar-coat these things."

This is the discourse of the Jesuits by which many simple Christians are taken in and led astray. For their sake, I will answer the main points of the Jesuits' question and discuss them only briefly, without offering a lengthy explanation, since this question deals with issues that have already been answered abundantly over the course of many years, and it is not to be regarded as worthy of a prolonged farewell.

But with God's help, I will attempt to demonstrate two things:

First, that the question posed by the Jesuits should not be given any weight, nor should anyone stumble over it, much less become a papist over it.

Second, that, although such an argument is practically unworthy of a response, nevertheless we can quite easily and even superfluously demonstrate how and where the right Church and religion were preserved before Luther.

The First Part of the Answer

The question posed by the Jesuits should not be given any weight and is almost unworthy of a response.

The apostle Paul, in his Second Epistle to his young disciple Timothy, chapter two, verse 23, prescribed the following rule: "Avoid foolish and useless questions, for you know that they only cause strife."

If the Jesuits were continually mindful of such a rule, they would surely stay at home with their question. For it is a truly foolish and useless question which only causes strife, without any certainty behind it. So that this may be clearly demonstrated and properly understood, let the Christian reader pay close attention to the following points:

First, the Jesuits' question is vain and of little use. For even if I did not know how to answer it, it would not hurt my salvation in the least. And if I know how to answer it, it still helps me very little for salvation.

Not knowing doesn't hurt, because it is enough that I am certain of what I am to believe, based on the Holy Scripture and the clear letters, even if I do not know exactly where and in what place the Christian Church has always existed. For if I demonstrate, article by article, that the Lutheran faith conforms to the Holy Scripture, that is sufficient. And it follows inevitably that this faith has always existed in the world, for the truth is not destroyed, even if I do not know where and among which people such faith has been preserved. Let each one see to it that he discovers the right faith from the Holy Scriptures. Then he can rest and be certain of his salvation, even if he cannot clearly demonstrate which individuals believed before he did. "The just lives by his faith," says Habakkuk 2:4. Thus, if each one looks to God's Word and draws his faith from it as the only source, then that is enough. It is not necessary that he trouble himself over what other people or their forbears believed. For he who has the right faith is most certainly saved; not knowing where the right-believing Christians were in the past cannot harm him in the least.

In the same way, it helps very little for salvation if I know who believed before I did, for I must consider every religion in the light of Holy Scripture, to see if it agrees with the Word of God. It certainly does not follow that, because this religion has been taught for so many consecutive centuries, therefore it must be right. That would mean that the fantasies of the Jews and Turks are also right, since they have likewise been promoted and preserved for many centuries. Thus there is little benefit, and nothing can be established as certain if I happen to know that a certain religion has been promoted in many places and over the course of many centuries, since the Greeks, the Jews, the Turks, and the heathen can all likewise make this boast. What is truly important is that each faith be tested according to the rule of Holy Scripture. That is much more important than for a person to trouble himself over where and from whom such faith was received. For the former makes a person certain and is necessary, while the latter does no harm if one does not know it and helps little if one does.

All this can be explained quite conveniently with a common analogy. Imagine a territory in which, for a long time, nothing but cheap copper coins have been used for money. But God graciously permits a godly man to discover some fine old silver coins, although no one knows where they were hammered or cast. Surely no one would be so foolish as to prefer the copper coins and reject the silver simply because the copper had been in use for a long time, and no one knew where the silver coins had been minted or who had originally used them. For although these things are unknown, no harm is done. It is sufficient that the old coins that were rediscovered withstand the test, proving that they were minted from fine silver. Why should a person trouble himself over where they were cast and who used them before? This analogy can easily be applied to the condition of the papist church. She likewise minted fake copper coins from all sorts of human statutes and grew accustomed to them over a long period of time. But God gave Doctor Luther grace, whereby he rediscovered the fine old silver coinage of the apostolic faith and brought it into the light of day. If his doctrine is compared with the Holy Scriptures, it withstands the test. But the papal minions are not satisfied with this; they are unwilling to receive such noble treasure and such precious coins of the truth—although it withstands the test—unless one can first show them the answer to their question: "Where and in what place were these coins used beforehand and when did they enter circulation?" Is that not a truly useless and unnecessary question, utterly unworthy of a response? It is entirely sufficient that the Lutheran doctrine withstands the test of the Holy Scriptures, even if we cannot expressly demonstrate when and where it was preserved under the enduring darkness of the papacy.

Secondly, it is truly a maliciously crafted question, which has as its goal to turn Evangelical hearts away from the Holy Bible and to conceal the detestable papal errors under the guise of ancient custom. The clever foxes—the Jesuits—know that, if their doctrine is ever investigated in the light of Holy Scripture, it will quickly burn up and vanish into thin air like a piece of straw. That is why they are so afraid of the Bible. That is why they do not wish to concede that the average person should read the Holy Scriptures at home and meditate on them diligently. John Eck himself, a renowned papist theologian from Ingolstadt, acknowledges that "the Lutheran religion can be opposed well enough from the ancient

Fathers, but not from the Holy Scripture." Albert Pighius loudly laments that, with Luther, one must begin one's argument from the Holy Scripture[2], thus clearly demonstrating that our doctrine has a deep and firm foundation in the Bible.

This fact is not lost on the Jesuits, for, when they want to provide the basis for the papist interpretation, they do not begin with the Bible; they maintain a stony silence in that regard. Instead, they ramble on about the name "Catholic," the succession of priests, the miracles of the saints, the unity and the long history of their Church, etc. Now, when an Evangelical Christian hears all this, he should immediately recognize it as a deceptive ploy and as a work of Satan, who, by means of such little arguments, would gladly take the Bible out of the picture and wrest from our hands the clear Word of God on which our doctrine rests. For he knows good and well that he cannot deceive us if we set our thoughts only on the revealed Word, which demonstrates sufficiently that the papist faith is wrong and cannot stand.

For example, a simple man can readily understand that the doctrine of purgatory is inane and man-made. For he finds not a single letter about it in the Holy Scripture. Instead, he finds that only two places are mentioned, heaven and hell, where the souls of those who die are immediately conveyed.

Anyone who reads and considers the institution of the Holy Supper can easily comprehend that it is wrong to rob simple Christians of the consecrated cup, as the second half of the Holy Supper. For the Lord Christ commanded, not only to eat the bread, but to drink the wine, when He says to all adult Christians, represented by the apostles, "Eat, drink of it all of you. This do in remembrance of Me, etc."

Anyone who searches the Holy Scriptures will at once find passages saying that man is to worship God alone and should place

2 l. 1. de Eccles. Hier. c. 4.

all his hope and trust in God alone. Therefore, it must be wrong when the papists also want people to call upon the saints who have died and to set their hope on the saints' help and intercession. For no such command or example or promise is to be found in Holy Scripture.

The Mass is considered to be the highest form of worship under the papacy, and yet there is not a single passage to be found in which anyone is commanded to sacrifice the body of Christ in the Supper. Nor is there any promise that such hearing of the Mass is to serve us for the forgiveness of sins. On what, then, is faith to be founded? On what should faith depend?

Paul expressly writes in 1 Cor. 7:9, "It is better to marry than to burn." And in 1 Tim. 3:25, "A bishop must be blameless, the husband of one wife, who has obedient children, etc." He thereby indicates clearly enough that marriage is not forbidden to the priests, and yet, in the papist church, it is considered wrong.

Paul also writes in many places that through the works of the Law no man can be saved, and yet, what this means for the papists is that good works earn salvation, and one should place his hope in them.

It is a notorious article in the Roman religion that the pope is the vicar of the Lord Christ and the successor of the apostle Peter. But where does one find even the slightest proof for this anywhere in the Holy Scriptures? No, we are supposed to believe everything the pope tells us to believe as if God Himself had said it!

They teach that no one can be certain that he has obtained the forgiveness of sins and that he is a child of eternal salvation. That is a truly terrible doctrine, which removes all the power of the Sacraments, of the Absolution, and of the promises, and brings with it nothing but grief and doubt, whereas the doctrine inspired by God is supposed to serve as a powerful comfort and a trusty salve for a bad conscience.

All this is so crystal clear that every Christian can readily understand what is true and what to believe. The hellish enemy knows this very well, which is why he seeks, through the Jesuits, to lead us away little by little from diligently considering the divine Word, toward the papist abomination. He puts on a show about the long history and the wide reach of the Roman Church. He demands that we tell him where our doctrine was before Luther's time and employs other similar sophistry. So take note, you Evangelical Christians, of this crafty little trick of Satan. Do not be infatuated with such syllogisms, which are a cover for all the papist errors. Remain with the Word of God, for it is a lamp to our feet (Psa. 119:105) that gives certainty and powerful comfort. Search the Scriptures, in which you will find eternal life (John 5:39). Take the articles of the papist religion and hold them up, one by one, to God's Word (especially before you get involved with the papists) to see which religion follows the Scriptures. Then the question—how and where the Christian Church was preserved—will surely answer itself.

The best advice is this: If a Jesuit tries to lay hold of you with the above-stated question, then answer his question with a question of your own. Say, "Friend, first tell me this: Where is it commanded in God's Word that I should call upon the saints, believe in purgatory, hear Mass, be saved by good works, receive the Lord's Supper under only one kind, buy indulgences, make pilgrimages, and do similar things?" If the Jesuit allows you to discuss any of these articles with him on the basis of Scripture, you have already won half the battle and can quickly stop his mouth. If he doesn't, he will have to resort to his usual excuse: "The Scriptures are too hard to understand. The Bible is a book for heretics. Everyone twists it however he wishes. The interpretation must be sought among the Fathers and the Councils. The Scriptures may be accepted, but only as the Roman Church understands them. Since there is no other judge, one should consult the pope. He does not err, etc." Thus he gives himself away, and you already see the fangs of the evil foe coming out, who would gladly lead you away from God's Word, the only means of salvation, which has been given to us clearly enough and for this very reason, that we should understand it and test all things by it. This is why he writhes and resists so vehemently. This is also why the crafty question of the Jesuits is not worth answering, unless they have first agreed to discuss the matter with you, article by article, on the basis of Holy Scripture, which alone makes certain.

Thirdly, it is also a shameless question. For they know very well how the popes persecuted those who believed rightly before Luther came along, and suppressed the truth with cunning and might. They even blotted out most of the books of those who opposed them. This is why they are so shameless with their questions and demand to know in short order who has previously followed our faith, because it is not unknown to them how those who believed rightly were persecuted and slain. It is as if a tyrannical ruler had kept the mouths of his subjects bound shut for a long time, so that they didn't dare speak publicly against his tyranny, or else faced banishment from his country. Then he demands an answer to the question, "Can you name anyone from years past who objected to anything in my government?" Everyone can see that this is pure deception and shameless whitewashing. It is no different with the papists. For, since they know that the truth was previously obscured under thick darkness and that pious Christians had to hide themselves, they resort so shamelessly to their question, "Where did the Christian Church sojourn before the time of Luther?"

Besides that, it should really be sufficient for all peace-loving, faithful Christians that we present and irrefutably prove our doctrine from the clear Word of God. Nevertheless, the Jesuits are not content with that. Nor are they willing to recognize our doctrine as right and Christian until and unless they can first be shown where it was preserved before the days of Luther. This is all a truly shameless business—no different than if someone were unwilling to believe that the Hebrew Bible is the true Bible, because it cannot be shown with certainty where and in what place it was hidden and preserved during the Babylonian captivity.

Fourthly, it is a truly Pharisaical question. For the Jesuits now make practically the same argument against the true religion as the Pharisees made against the doctrine of Christ and the apostles long ago. They considered Christ's doctrine to be something new (Mark 1:27). They refused to accept it, because their old traditions and the additions of the fathers were made invalid by it. Without any hesitation, they boasted of their antiquity and their origins, as the modern Jesuits also do. They held a similar discourse and posed similar questions: "Tell us, apostles, where did anyone teach like this in former times? Who, prior to Jesus the crucified, taught that the Law of Moses and circumcision and other traditions were to be abrogated? We sit in Moses' seat. The authority and the understanding were entrusted to us to interpret the Scriptures of the prophets. Our synagogue and doctrine have endured for many hundreds of years. No one has ever taught anything other than what we teach about the kingdom of the Messiah, righteousness, and the understanding of the Ten Commandments. Therefore, either our religion is right, or it would have to follow that no Church and no true faith ever existed before on earth, since no one has ever heard of any except for our Pharisaical doctrine. But, tell us the place. Name for us the people who formerly agreed with you and rejected our understanding. Do not talk to us about your miracles, for the false prophets can do miracles, too. Indeed, it is a sure sign of deception when miracles are done to confirm an entirely new, unheard-of doctrine which goes against the old Mosaic religion, etc."

Without any doubt, the old Pharisees must have argued in these and similar ways against the apostles and their doctrine.

Whatever reply the Jesuits make to this Pharisaical objection, we wish to throw the very same reply back at them when it comes to their question. But there is no more convenient answer than this: It is sufficient that the doctrine of the apostles agrees with the prophecies and writings of the prophets. Also irrefutable is the fact that there were always godly Jews who did not endorse the errors of the Pharisees, even if one could not expressly name them or the places where they lived. In the same way, we say that one should be satisfied with the fact that our religion agrees with the Holy Scriptures. Thus, there is no doubt that there have always been some who have followed it, even if, on account of the pope's tyranny and persecution, they have not always been known or been allowed to practice their religion openly.

Fifthly, the Jesuits' question cannot provide a sure and certain conclusion. For even if we could not expressly name the location of the ancient church or the individuals who believed rightly, it would still not follow on that account that no true Church existed before Luther. For a thing can certainly exist and be preserved, even if one does not know where and how it was preserved. *Ab ignorantia rei ad negationem rei non licet argumentari.* "Let no one conclude that a thing does not exist simply because he is ignorant of it," say the scholars. If I wanted to deny that paradise ever existed simply because the place where it was cannot be precisely identified, wouldn't everyone consider that a foolish and a shameless conclusion? In the same way, it does not follow that no spiritual paradise—no Christian Church—existed before Luther, even if we cannot at this time specifically identify its location, especially since the true believers have never lived together in a single place, but are scattered here and there, not under a peaceful existence, but under the tyranny and persecution of the pope.

The prophet Elijah also thought at one time that he was the only one left of all the godly in the kingdom of Israel, for he didn't know the other God-fearing Jews, nor could he know them, since they were oppressed and had to remain hidden. Nevertheless, a Church still existed even in the midst of the idolatrous kingdom of Israel, for God Himself said in 1 Kings 19:18 that He would allow seven thousand to remain in Israel; namely, all the knees that did not bow to Baal and every mouth that did not kiss him. Elijah's logic did not avail before the divine majesty: "I, Elijah, do not know the location of the right worship of God, nor do I know any individual who has not followed after Baal. Therefore, there is no true Church left anywhere in Israel." So the reasoning of the Jesuits is also flawed when they assert that, before Luther, there were no true believers who opposed the papist abominations, because no one can say for certain who or where they were. It is sufficient for us to know that the apostolic Church will always exist, and that the gates of hell will not overcome it (Mat. 16:18), as the Lord Christ also promised that He would be with us, even to the end of the age (Mat. 28:20). On the basis of this promise, we are certain that, even in the midst of the idolatrous papacy, the Lord God has had His true lambs and has also preserved His seven thousand, as in the kingdom of Israel, even if, with Elijah, we do not recognize them or know their names.

In the sixth and last place, this question and the whole argument based upon it springs from a false hypothesis and interpretation. For the papists pretend—and would have everyone believe—that the Christian Church must always be visible, in such a way that one can identify its location and readily distinguish the individuals who belong to it from others who do not. It is supposed to be as tangible as the kingdom of France or the city of Venice, whose location is clearly known and whose inhabitants are readily identified, as Bellarmine writes[3].

But this is entirely wrong. The Christian Church sometimes loses its appearance and becomes practically invisible. She is

3 lib. 3. de Ecclesia cap. 2.

forced to hide, being scattered here and there. This can be explained and demonstrated quite easily, both with the prophecies of the divine Scriptures and with many examples from the Old and New Testaments.

Concerning the prophecies, our dear Savior Himself declares in Luke 18:8 that, when He comes—namely, for judgment—almost no faith will be found any longer on the earth. He is not referring to the *fidem miraculorum,* the faith to do miracles, of which Paul speaks in 1 Cor. 13:1, but about the *fidem articulorum,* the faith of assenting to the right doctrine, as He also prophesies in Mat. 24 that false prophets will arise and will lead many into error—even the elect, if it were possible. But if the Christian Church were to be thoroughly and visibly flourishing at all times, as the papists imagine, then there is no room for this prophecy of Christ, saying that He will find no faith on the earth. The apostle Paul similarly prophesied in 2 The. 2:3 about a widespread apostasy that is to take place in the last days, 1 Tim. 4:1. Therefore, the papists from Reims also write: *"Paulo ante finem mundo externus status Ecclesiae cessabit,* ἀποστασία *passim obtinebit,"* that is, "Shortly before the end of the world, the external condition of the Church (which consists in public practice) will cease, and apostasy will gain the upper hand." This means nothing else but that the Christian Church is to become invisible. Likewise, John declared beforehand in his Revelation that the woman, that is, the Christian Church, would have to flee to the wilderness (Rev. 12:6), that the inhabitants of the earth would be persecuted by the beast (Rev. 13:15), and that those who do not worship the image of the beast would be killed (Rev. 13:16). From all this it is sufficiently clear that the Christian Church will be so oppressed under the Antichrist that she is forced to hide and be scattered here and there.

Concerning the examples, they are familiar enough from the Holy Scriptures. Where was the public, visible Church when all the people sinned on Mt. Sinai and worshiped the golden calf (Exo. 32:10, 17)? Where was the right service of God publicly taking place in the kingdom of Israel at the time of Elijah? Where and in what location were the true believers to be found at the time of the Pharisees, many years before Christ's coming in the flesh? Name the place, name the individuals who publicly rejected the detestable errors in the doctrine of the Pharisees. No one can do it, and yet it surely does not follow that, under Aaron's idolatry, at the time of Elijah, and among the Pharisaical company before the birth of Christ, there were no pious, godly hearts in whom the true Church could have been preserved. For, especially at the time of the Pharisees, there was no public religion in the whole world practiced more devoutly than the heathen, distorted Jewish religion—that is, the religion of the Pharisees—against which the Lord Christ often directed His sermons and demonstrated clearly enough that it was distorted, leading men away from heaven. Thus it inevitably follows that, either there was absolutely no true Church remaining at that time, or the true believers were hidden among the company of the Pharisees. Likewise, we know from Church history how, under the ten persecutions, the Christians were so oppressed that they were often unable to practice their religion publicly. Nor can any definite location be identified where they lived, but at times they were forced to hole up in the wilderness; at times they hid in the clefts of the rocks; at times they were tucked away amongst the heathen. We also know how, later, at the time of the Arian heresy, when the whole world accepted the Arian throng, the truly Catholic Christians were persecuted and were unable to remain in any defined place.

Therefore, since it follows incontrovertibly from this that the Christian Church is sometimes invisible, especially at a time of universal persecution, and since the same sort of tyranny was exercised against the true believers under the darkness of the papacy, everyone should be able to see that the Jesuits' question is a truly useless and shameless question when they want us to specifically name the place and the individuals who followed our doctrine. For such a question only applies to the visible Church when she is in a good state and is free to practice openly. But the pope has banned and forbidden this for a long time, with great violence, to all who will not accept his authority. Thus, when someone asks for the location of the oppressed Church under the papacy, it is as absurd as if someone were to ask where to find that which is hidden or where to see that which is invisible. For these things are contradictory, to be oppressed and invisible, and yet to be openly seen and located.

Let this serve as a summary of our answer to the question posed by the Jesuits, wherein we have briefly demonstrated: (1) That it is a vain question, since no one is harmed if he does not know how to answer it, and is helped very little if he does. (2) That it is a malicious question, posed for the sole purpose of turning us away from considering the Holy Scriptures, thus leading us into the particular abomination of the papists. (3) That it is a shameless question, since they know that the pope has oppressed the true believers. Apart from this, it is sufficient that we prove our doctrine from the Holy Scripture. (4) That it is a Pharisaical question, since the same sort of questioning was also aimed at the apostles. (5) That it provides no reliable or certain conclusion, since it does not follow that there was no Church simply because we may not know where it was located. (6) That it is based on a false premise, as if the Church were always visible and recognizable, while the opposite can very easily be demonstrated with prophecies and examples.

The Second Part of the Answer

One can indeed demonstrate how and where the true Church and religion were preserved before Luther's time.

Two things must be considered in this regard:
First, how our apostolic faith was preserved under the papacy.
Second, who the members of the true Church were.

Concerning the first point, we offer this brief answer: **Our apostolic faith has been preserved at all times in the Bible, that is, the Holy Scripture.** For we have not invented any new doctrine. On the contrary, we have studied the doctrine of God's Word, as we can easily demonstrate from one article to the next. For since it is undeniable that the true Catholic religion is written in the Bible, and that, through God's providence, this Holy Bible was preserved even in the midst of the papacy, it follows incontrovertibly that the truth, that is, the apostolic faith, has never been lost or entirely wiped out. In order that this may be understood even more clearly, let us offer the following syllogism:

Where the Bible remains, there the true religion also is and remains, as that which is thoroughly defined therein.

But the Bible remained and was preserved even in the midst of the darkness of the papacy.

Therefore, the true religion remained and was preserved, not being entirely lost or destroyed in the midst of the papacy.

Furthermore, the Holy Scripture was not somehow buried in the ground before Luther's time, nor was it tucked away in a cleft of rock, so that no one could have read it or heard of it. At a minimum, the Gospels and the apostolic lessons were read to the people every week, although the monks then added their own interpretations and stories.

In addition, there is no doubt that many godly hearts also studied on their own and diligently searched the Scriptures, which does not occur without bearing fruit, since the Word of God never returns empty (Isa. 55:11).

From this it is now clear, first, that our doctrine never became extinct, since it was always preserved in the Holy Scripture; second, that it was also publicly set before the people as often as the Biblical text was read in the Church; third, that it was also received in the home when God-fearing hearts diligently read God's Word in their houses, since this is never a fruitless endeavor.

The state of things under the papacy was just like things were at the time of the Pharisaic corruptions. At the time of the Pharisees, the right doctrine was preserved in the Scriptures of Moses and the prophets, to which Father Abraham (Luke 16:29) and the Lord Christ attest (Mat. 23:2). In the same way, under the papacy, although many detestable things were promoted, nonetheless the Holy Bible, and thus also the apostolic faith contained therein, remained at all times and was kept perfectly safe.

Herman Hugo objects[4]: "All heretics could likewise claim that their religion has also been preserved and promoted at all times, since the Bible has always been read."

Answer: It is one thing to make a bare claim. It is another thing to back up one's claim with sound reasoning and truth. The heretics' claim is false, because their doctrine does not agree with the Scriptures. Our claim is right, because our doctrine is grounded in the Holy Scriptures. Do the Jesuits deny this? Fine! Then they should journey with us into the Holy Bible and set aside this use-

4 l. 3. de vera fide capessenda p. 174.

less question. The heretics also claim that the ancient teachers of the Church agree with them. Do the papists, then, wish to abandon their evidence from the ancient teachers of the Church?

Secondly, concerning the Christian Church and her members, it is also easy to point out where she was before Luther's time; namely, **in the midst of the papacy**. Why? Because it is written in 2 The. 2:4 that the Antichrist will sit in the temple of God, that is, in the Christian Church. That the Roman pope is that very Antichrist follows from the fact that he has sat in the temple of God. Consequently, the house of the Lord, that is, the Christian Church, has existed in the midst of the papacy, since no one but the pope could have ruled over God's temple.

Some may further ask who the individuals were who did not properly belong to the papist church, but to the catholic, apostolic Church. We would certainly not be obligated to answer such a question, since the true Christians were mostly scattered here and there and remained hidden. Nevertheless, we charitably offer this reliable answer: There were four distinct groups of true Christians who are all to be considered members of the true, apostolic Church.

In the first group we place **the little children who have been baptized**. For although the Sacrament of Holy Baptism has been tainted with many human embellishments, it has remained perfectly intact with regard to its essence and effect, in such a way that, even through the papists' Baptism, the little children were cleansed from sin, united to Christ, and received as true members of the apostolic church on earth. Accordingly, even if no one could name anyone beyond the baptized little children, we would have already demonstrated that the Christian Church did not completely and utterly perish under the papacy. Thus we may conclude:

Where baptized and reborn little children are, there, too, is the true, apostolic Church.

Under the papacy there were always baptized and reborn little children.

Therefore, the apostolic Church always truly existed under the papacy.

An inept priest will object, "We couldn't prove that the little children were devoted to our faith. The Calvinists would assert the same thing about their religion, etc."

Answer: We are discussing the little children, not as confessors of our faith, but as members of the true Church. For the papists say that the Church must have entirely perished before Luther's time, since the Evangelical religion was not yet in full swing. To that we say, their reasoning is flawed. For the true Church at the very least could have been preserved in the baptized children, as true members. But with regard to the acceptance and confession of the true religion, we do not attempt to prove and demonstrate that from the example of the children, but from the example of other godly people.

In the second group are **dying Christians**, many of whom undoubtedly turned to Christ alone as their Savior shortly before their death, no longer relying on their own works or on the merit of the saints. For they found, in practice, that such a doctrine could not offer any firm comfort or a peaceful conscience, and so, like stubble, it went up in flames and vanished from their hearts. Each one of us, too, is persuaded that, if God wanted to enter into judgment with us, we, with our good works, could never stand. Therefore, we are afraid—even terrified—when we hear something about the final, strict judgment of God. Thus there is no doubt that many of them, in the throes of death, looked to Christ alone and His merit, to which they were also directed in *Hortulus Animae*, a prayer book that includes many beautiful little prayers which have often been prayed with the dying, directing them only to the merit of Christ. The same holds true in the Agenda of Mainz (fol. 71) and of Salzburg (fol. 10). Martinus Eisengrein, former professor at Ingolstadt, with the approval of the theological faculty, wrote an especially helpful book about this topic, namely, how, in the papacy, one should comfort the dying and direct them only to the merit of Christ. Thus, when Duke George of Saxony was in the throes of death, a crucifix was held before his eyes as he was told, "Straight paths make for good runners!"[5] This was a favorite saying of the duke, and thereby he was directed to Christ alone.

Clemens Schau, chaplain at Eisleben, also bears witness in the *Catalogus testium veritatis*[6] as he tells how he stood at the deathbed of Archbishop Ernest of Magdeburg, where he was chaplain at that time. Two Franciscans were also there, one of whom said, "Be of good cheer, dear prince! We will share with Your Grace, not only our good works, but also those of the entire Minorite order. Surely with that you will be able to stand before God's judgment seat and be saved." To this the archbishop replied, "Certainly not! I want nothing to do with your works. Only the works of my Lord Christ will do. On them will I rely." The secretary of Pope Paul V tells the story of the Roman Emperor, Charles V, how the Bishop of Toledo himself wrote to the pope in Rome, saying that Emperor Charles spoke these words shortly before he died: "I think that the doctrine of the Lutherans concerning justification is the true and Scriptural teaching." Some recount similar things concerning Emperor Maximilian II, how the Neopolitan Bishop Lambertus Graterus came to visit him before his death. But he would not allow him to come in to him until the bishop promised to speak with him about nothing else but the merit and bloody sweat of Christ. The bishop proceeded to do this and preached a beautiful sermon about the benefits of Christ. Afterwards, when asked if he was prepared to die in this faith and comfort, the emperor answered, "I will not do otherwise."

---

5 *Gerade zu giebt gute Renner.*

6 tom. 2. lib. 19. pag. 905.

This, then, is the second group of true Christians, namely, those who, in times of tribulation and on their deathbed, have recognized the imperfection of their works and the false doctrine of the papists, who found themselves fleeing with their faith to the Lord Christ alone. From this it is even more apparent how inane is the outburst of an inept priest who has latched onto Lessius and pretends, "It cannot be proven that the dying papists became Lutherans. One could just as easily claim that they became Turks!" For the first assertion has already been proven, especially as it applies to the article concerning the basis of salvation and the imperfection of works. The second is a crass prevarication; not a single indication of apostasy to the Turkish religion can be produced, while we can certainly demonstrate the opposite, that many dying Christians, through the testimony of their own conscience and the content of their prayers, have come to recognize the imperfection of their works and have set their confidence on the merits of Christ alone, and thus have died as good Evangelicals.

In the third group we place **the secret and scattered Christians**. For just as, at the time of Elijah and of the Pharisees, there were only false teachers in the kingdom of Israel and Judaism was the religion of the day, nevertheless many thousands of pious souls were hidden among them—believers who did not endorse the abominations, but held to the true doctrine in their hearts. They were also particularly preserved by God, so that they neither had to play the hypocrite nor give up their life. Thus it is also certain that, in the papacy, many God-fearing hearts have always been found who have recognized the truth and have not given their consent to the pope's abominations and tyranny. For even if they never openly preached against it, since they were forced to live in fear of persecution, keeping in mind that one should not willingly place one's life in danger, nevertheless they held onto the true faith in their hearts, nor did they bend the knee before the Roman Baal. Indeed, there was plenty of complaining in the papacy, even before Luther, over the great abuses and all kinds of errors that crept in, one after another, so that pious hearts often and in many places longed for a Christian Reformation. That is why, as soon as Luther began to preach and to write against indulgences, many of them were sincerely happy about it and gave thanks to God that their longings had been heard and that a man had now come who would undertake to accomplish the long-awaited work of Reformation. In the same way, there are many today under the papacy who think very little of the pope's authority, of purgatory, of the Mass, and of the merit of good works, and thus they are one with us, even though they remain in the papacy, either out of fear or because the Lutheran doctrine in other articles has been made so repugnant to them by the Jesuits. The apostolic Church was, in large part, preserved before Luther's time, as it was at the time of Elijah and of the Pharisees, in such secret, pious, and simple Christians.

In the fourth and final group we place **the holy martyrs and the public confessors of the Evangelical truth**. Such people have always been found in the papacy, for there has never been a lack of God-fearing, sincere Christians who have opposed the pope and have fearlessly pointed out his abominations to the people, even though it meant that they should soon lose their lives, that their books should be burned and their names blotted out, to the point that it is impossible to know about all the martyrs who have died under the papacy. But the histories of Magdeburg tell of a good many of them, as any diligent reader can investigate for himself.

For, first of all, there were entire congregations that opposed the pope on many points and challenged his doctrine, as the Waldensians—otherwise known as the poor men of Lyons—did for many consecutive years, and almost continually. They rejected man-made rules, purgatory, the Mass, pilgrimages, the celibacy of the priests, monastic orders, and other papist articles of faith, ordering their religion instead from the Holy Scripture. This is documented in various sources[7]. Next to the Waldensians were the Greek churches, which, likewise, were never willing to recognize the pope as a universal bishop and vicar of Christ, nor do they even now recognize him as such. Therefore, every year, on Quadragesima [8]Sunday, they excommunicate him and place him under the ban as an open heretic.

Secondly, there have also been many pious emperors, kings, and princes who were unwilling to submit to the pope's abominations and activities. Emperor Henry IV opposed Pope Gregory VII. Emperor Fredrick II rebuked the pope for usurping undue authority for himself, wanting everyone to fear him as a god. King Philip of France refused to yield any authority to the pope in secular matters. Emperor Louis IV considered Pope John XXII to be a heresiarch, a ruler of heretics. Other Roman emperors also belong in this number, such as Otto IV, Henry VII, etc., King John and King Edward III of England, Charlemagne and Louis XII of France, as well as other prominent lords and princes who took no pleasure in the pope's doctrine or life.

Finally, there have at all times been steadfast teachers who defended the Evangelical truth and were consequently put to death by the pope, as Huss and Savonarola experienced. If anyone wishes to read stories like these and learn more about them, he should consult the *Catalogus testium veritatis,* in which an account is given, century by century through the ages, what kind of individuals opposed the pope and how the true Evangelical faith was always preached and advanced, even in the midst of darkness. I would direct the conscientious reader to this resource.

---

7 *Catalogus testium veritais,* part. 2. lib. 15.; Aeneas Sylvius in hist. Bohem. cap. 35.; Sleidanus lib. 16.; Poplinerius in hist. Fr. l. 1. edit. Anno 1581. fol. 6. 7.; and Thuanus in the fifth book of his histories.

8 i.e., Invocavit

Herman Hugo[9] makes a foolish, simplistic objection when he writes, "Clearly no one confessed the Lutheran faith before Luther, because Lutheranism didn't exist before Luther." For the doctrine *per se* is one thing; the Lutheran label is another. Our doctrine has always existed, although it was not always called Lutheran. In the same way the true Christians in the enduring Arian controversy were called homoousians—a word which first came into existence at that time. Should one conclude from that that the doctrine of the *homoousia* of the Son of God was neither acknowledged nor confessed before that time?

And so we have now demonstrated, first, that our doctrine was preserved at all times under the papacy in the Holy Bible.

Second, that the true Church existed among the papists, since the pope was sitting in the temple of God.

Third, that true members of the Christian Church have always existed, for there have always been (1) baptized little children; (2) pious dying Christians; (3) secret Christians; (4) public confessors of the truth, including whole congregations, emperors, kings, teachers and preachers who, although they sometimes err on this or that point, nevertheless agree with us in the majority of articles, unlike the papists, who cannot point to any who, over the course of a thousand or more years, taught in all articles as the Jesuits of today are accustomed to teach. A more detailed account of this can be given in another place, at another time.

But to You, O Lord Jesus Christ, who alone are the Head of Your Church, who alone are the Way and the Truth, we fervently pray: Preserve Your flock among us. Give strength to Your Word. Subdue the Jesuits, and graciously protect us from their seductive apostasy, that Your name may be hallowed, Your kingdom extended, and Your will accomplished, both here in time and there in eternity. To you, with the Father and the Holy Spirit, be glory, honor, and praise, forever and ever. Amen.

---

9 l. 3. p. 175.

Also available from Repristination Press:

Johannes Bugenhagen, *The Public Confession of Johannes Bugenhagen of Pomerania: Concerning the Sacrament of the Body and Blood of Christ* (1528), paperback, 210 pages, ISBN 1-891469-70-3, $16.95.

Johannes Bugenhagen, *The Annotations of Johannes Bugenhagen on Ten Epistles of Paul,* paperback, 298 pages, ISBN 1-891469-72-X, $24.95.

Johann Gerhard, *A Comprehensive Explanation of Holy Baptism and the Lord's Supper* (1610), paperback, 468 pages, ISBN 1-891469-66-5, $27.97.

Johann Gerhard, *Annotations on the First Six Chapters of St. Paul's Epistle to the Romans* (1645), paperback, 294 pages, ISBN 1-891469-67-3. $19.99,

Johann Gerhard, *Annotations on the Revelation of St. John the Theologian* (1643), paperback, 218 pages, ISBN 1-891469-69-X, $24.95.

Johann Gerhard, *On the Legitimate Interpretation of Holy Scripture* (1610), paperback, 130 pages, ISBN 1-891469-68-1, $14.95.

Nicolaus Hunnius, *Principia Theologiae Fanaticae (1619): The Principles of the Fanatic Theology*, paperback, 106 pages, ISBN 1-891469-27-4, $12.99.

To order directly from Repristination Press, please send a check or money order for the cost of the book plus $3.00 per book for shipping and handling to: Repristination Press, 716 HCR 3424 E, Malone, Texas 76660.

81815187R00066

Made in the USA
Middletown, DE
28 July 2018